AL-FAUZ AL-KABIR FI USUL AL-TAFSIR

(The Principles of Qur'an Commentary)

by

Shah Waliyullah

Translated by

G. N. Jalbani

KITAB BHAVAN
NEW DELHI-110002

Kitab Bhavan
Exporters & Emporters
1784, Kalan Mahal,
Darya Ganj, New Delhi-110002

Phone : 23274686, 23277392-93
E-mail : nasri@vsnl.com
Fax : 91-11-23263383
Website : www.kitabbhavan.com

ISBN : 81-7151-231-3

First Edition 1985
Reprint 1997
Reprint 1999
Reprint 2004

Published in India by :
Nusrat Ali Nasri for Kitab Bhavan
1784, Kalan Mahal,
Darya Ganj, New Delhi-110002

Printed in India at :
Lahoti Fine Art Press
1711, Suiwalan, Darya Ganj,
New Delhi-110002

THANKSGIVING

God's countless favours are on this humble servant, and the greatest of them is His assistance to His servant in understanding the Holy Qur'ān. The favour of the Holy Prophet on this weak community are many, the greatest of them being the teaching of the Holy Qur'ān. He taught the Qur'ān to the first generation which conveyed the teaching to the second generation; this is how the process continued without interruption till a portion of it reached this humble servant as well. O, God, the Most Merciful, Shower, by thy Mercy, Thy best blessings and benedictions on the noble Prophet, our chief, master and intercessor; also on his family, his companions and the learned of his Ummah.

PREFACE

Al-Fauz Al-Kabīr Fī Usūl Al-Tafsīr is among Shāh Walīyullāh's important works and presumably the best compilation ever prepared on the subject. The author's approach to the study of the Qur'ān is independent and in conformity with the exigencies of logic. It helps in clearing the cobwebs of misconception which sometimes crop up in the minds of non-Muslim readers; it also helps commentators in tiding over difficulties which they occasionally come across in comprehending the Holy Book. Shāh Walīyullāh has, by his direct approach, been able to show how judiciously the traditions about the Prayers have been inferred from the Book of God. It was with this in view that he compiled this treatise; he has himself given an indication of this somewhere in the body of the text.[1]

The study of this treatise before undertaking the study of the Qur'an will prove highly useful. Its original Persian text has already been translated into Arabic and Urdu, and a strong need was felt also to have an English version. This need is sought to be fulfilled in this humble effort. It will be worthwhile both for the teacher and the student to consult it by way of an introduction to the study of the Holy Qur'ān.

G. N. Jalbani
Formerly Professor and Head of
the Department of Arabic,
University of Sind

1. Al-Khair-Al-Kathīr p. 87

CONTENTS

INTRODUCTION

Walīyullāh b Abu-ur-Rahīm (on both of whom may God's grace be) says that when a window of the Book of God was opened on him, he felt impelled to produce a small treatise to incorporate useful points which could help friends in understanding the Qur'ān. He hopes, with the mercy of God, that by simply being aware of these rules, the students of Qur'ān would find a wide opening before them. Otherwise they would not be able to obtain as accurate and logical account as is given here even if they were to spend their whole life on the commentaries or work under the commentators who incidently are very few in the present age. I have named this treatise as Al-Fauz-ul-Kabīr Fī Usūl Al-Tafsīr, and have no support except that of God. On Him I rely, and He is enough for me. He is the best protector.

The discussion is confined to five chapters. First chapter deals with the explanation of the five sciences enunciated in the Qur'ān, appearing to be the very purpose of the Revelation. The second chapter relates to the reasons for observing secrecy in the arrangement of the Qur'ānic verses in the context of the level of intelligence of the people of the age, and the explanation of those reasons. Third chapter relates to the beauties implicit in the arrangement and the elucidation, as far as is humanly possible and of its wonderful style. The fourth chapter refers to the exigency and a solution to the differences among the Companions and their immediate followers. The fifth chapter gives an account of the commentaries of the rarities (Ghāraib) of the Qur'ān, and the reasons of the revelation of various verses to the extent necessary for a commentator. Any attempt to go deep into the science of commentary without being in possession of this information is certainly forbidden!

1. The fifth chapter is not included here. It is in the form of separate treatise named by Shāh Sāhib as Fath Al-Khabīr.

THE FIRST CHAPTER

EXPLANATION OF FIVE SCIENCES

The significance underlying the arrangement of the Holy Qur'ān is covered by a set of five sciences, as follows:

1. The Science of Injunctions (Aḥkām): This includes the Incumbent, the Recommended, the Approved, the Disapproved and the Forbidden, covering worships, social dealings, household economy, and state politics. Its discussion is the responsibility of jurists.

2. The Science of Disputation (Mukhasimah): This deals with the four misguided sects, the Jews, the Christians, the Polytheists and the Hypocrites, and its discussion and analysis falls within the jurisdiction of dialecticians.

3. The Science of Divine Favours: This covers explanation of the creation of the Heavens and the Earth, of the perfect attributes of God and the guidance which the people received about necessities of life.

4. Fourth is the science covering the important events which God caused to take place, favouring the obedient and punishing the disobedient.

5. The fifth is the science which reminds human beings of Death, and what will follow it,— the Resurrection, the Gathering, the Reckoning, the Balance, the Paradise, and the Hell. A preacher must possess full knowledge of these sciences; he should be able to trace their connection with appropriate Traditions and sayings of the Holy Prophet.

The explanation of these sciences is provided in the style of speech of ancient Arabs and not in that of the moderns. Therefore, the procedure of the latter writers of being brief in selection of verses pertaining to the injunctions has not been followed. Similarly, unnecessary restrictions which is the technique of present day academicians have not been taken into consideration. In the case of verses which relate to Disputation, accepted principles and useful sermons – and not the order of demonstrations as is the fashion of the logicians – have been taken into consideration. While shifting from one problem to the other, suitability of the link between the pros and cons, as has been the practice of men of letters, has not been cared for. What God thought beneficial for His servants He revealed irrespective of what may precede and what may follow.

Generally, the commentators have linked every verse about Disputations and Injunctions with an event, and have taken that event as the cause of its revelation. In fact, the purpose underlying the revelation of the Qur'ān was the purification of the hearts of the people, repudiation of their corrupt beliefs and eradication of their evil actions. The presence of false beliefs in the minds of responsible people was the real reason for the revelation of verses of Disputations. The presence of corruption, wide-spread injustice and wrong-doing formed the basis of revelation of verses relating to Injunctions. Similarly, their failure to take notice of God's blessings for the obedient and punishments for the disobedient, also of Death and what is to follow it, became the cause of the revelation of the verses which remind and admonish. Particular events, for whose narration so much trouble has been taken by the commentators, have nothing to do with the revelation of the verses. There are, however, some verses where clear references have been made to certain events which had occurred during the Holy Prophet's life time or had happened before his advent. Undoubtedly, the hearer would like to know, in such cases, detailed account of the event concerned; his anxiety will not disappear without this. It is, therefore, necessary to explain these sciences in a manner as would not call for the narration of particular events.

The Science of Disputation

Disputation verses refer to the four misguided sects, the Polytheists, the Jews, the Christians and the Hypocrites. Disputation is done in two ways; firstly a clear exposure of the false belief, and its evil effects, and then its denunciation; secondly listing of doubts of these people, and their removal through demonstrativeness and oration.

Polytheists described themselves as "Aḥnāf" (seekers of truth), claiming to follow the religion of Abraham. Actually Ḥānāfi is one who follows the creed of Abraham and observes the rituals prescribed by him. These rituals include pilgrimage to Kaâba, keeping one's face towards it while saying prayers, bath after ceremonious uncleanliness, circumcision, and other virtuous acts dictated by sound nature. Additionally, they include observing sanctity of the months during which fighting is forbidden, veneration of the Sacred Mosque, observing prohibition of marriage with specifically listed relatives, slaughter of an animal by cutting its throat, of the camel at chest, sacrifice of animals particularly during the Hajj days. There are then offering of prayers, fast from early dawn to sunset, giving alms to the poor and orphans, rendering them help when in distress, maintenance of relationship; all these were prescribed in the religion of Abraham; and his followers upheld them. The Polytheists had generally abandoned them, and put an end to them. Again, unlawful murder, theft, adultery, usury and usurpation were forbidden by Abraham's creed, but the Polytheists indulged in these evil practices, having submitted completely to the evil in them (Nafs Ammārah).

It had been made incumbent on them – and their poetry testifies to this – to believe that there is God, that He is the Creator of the heavens and the earth, that He is the Administrator of the momentous events and has the power to send Messengers, that He will reward His servants for righteous deeds, that He determines important events, and even before they occur, and that the angels are His Servants, very near to him and are to be respected. But about all these, the Polytheists had in general created doubts, describing them improbable and showing no interest in comprehending them. Polytheism, belief in anthropomorphism, modification of Abraham's scroll, denial of the Hereafter, and terming the Holy Prophet's mission unbelievable, constituted main features of their deviation from the true religion of Abraham. In addition, they performed shameful deeds, indulged in injustice, wrong-doing, and corrupt practices, and wiped out every semblance of God's worship.

Polytheism

It means proving existence of attributes, as belong to God alone, in others also. For example, people generally held the belief that there did exist other beings besides God who possessed their own will to act freely as if to say "Be, and it happens". Or they accepted the existence of beings who possessed personal Knowledge not attainable through sense-organs, rationality, a dream, or an inspiration. They had the wrong notion that these beings could heal a sick, hurl a curse on a person, and, by expressing their displeasure, make a person poor, sick and unhappy, or otherwise could bestow mercy on a person which enabled him to lead a healthy, happy and pleasant life. These Polytheists did not associate anybody with God in the creation of substances and administration of important affairs. They did not believe that there existed power in any creature by which he could prevent God from doing the work, he decided to do. Their polytheism related to affairs peculiar to certain servants. They thought that just as a worldly lord could send his chosen officers to various parts of his country, vesting them with full powers to act freely in specific cases as long as they did not receive fresh instructions from him and their recommendations for those who sought redress were accepted by the worldly Lord, precisely in the same manner the Supreme Lord (God) conferred on some of His servants the role of divinity, and pleasure or displeasure of these servants of His had an influence on the fate of the people. Thus, they thought it was necessary to seek the nearness of these select so that their prayers become acceptable to the Absolute Ruler (God), also through the recommendations of these selected persons.

In view of this, the Polytheists decided to bow down before these beings, to offer sacrifices for them, to take an oath by their names, to seek help from their extraordinary powers (namely 'Be and it becomes'). They would carve their images from stone, copper, glass etc, and make the spirits of the dead focus of their deep attention. With the passage of time, these stone images became semblances of Diety for the ignorant. This is how the great confusion took birth.

Anthropomorphism (Tashbīh)

This means to prove the presence of human attributes in God. They would thus say that angels were God's daughters, and that He accepted intercession of His select servants made on behalf of the people even though otherwise He might not find them acceptable, just as sometimes do the worldly Kings in relation to their responsible officers. When they could not comprehend the true attributes of God such as Knowledge, and power of hearing and seeing, they started judging them also in the context of their own knowledge, and capacity of hearing and seeing. And this was how they went astray, taking God as corporal and boundable.

Change (Taḥrīf)

The story of the Change is that the children of Prophet Ismāil followed their grandfather Abrahim's Shariāh (law) till Āmr b. Luḥayy, may God curse him, appeared. He carved idols and made their worship compulsory for them. He also instituted superstitions, such as 'Bahīra', 'Sā'iba', 'Wasīla', 'Ḥām', 'Al-Iqtisamī lil Azlām' and many

1. Bahīra, a slit-ear she-camel or a she-camel let loose for free pasture. If a she-camel or other female domestic animal had a large number of youngs, she (or one of the offsprings) had been ear-slit and she was dedicated to a god. 'Sā'iba: on return in safety from journey or on recovery from illness, a she-camel was dedicated to a god and let loose for free pasture. Such she-camel was called Sā'iba. Wasilā: When an animal bore twins, certain sacrifices or dedications were made to idols. The animal so decicated was called Wasīla. Hām: A stallion camel dedicated to the gods, by certain rites. Al-Iqtisām bil Azlām: Division by arrows. The arrows were used for the division of meat by a sort of lottery or raffle. But the arrows were also used for divination, for ascertaining lucky or unlucky moments or learning the wishes of the heathen gods, as to whether man should undertake certain actions or not (See Allama Yūsuf Alī's English translation of the Holy Qurān, Vol. 1, pp. 271. 275).

others![1] This change took place three hundred years before the birth of the Holy Prophet.

In addition to these evil practices, they adhered to the traditions of their forefathers, and considered it as a decisive argument in their favour. The Prophets who had gone before had spoken about the Resurrection and the Gathering, but they had given no details, nor stated it as distinctly with all particulars as given in the Qur'ān (though rather very summarily). Since the Polytheists were not given detailed account of life after death, they considered the happening of Resurrection as impossible and far remote.

Even though these people acknowledged the prophethood of Prophets Abrahim, Ismāil, and also that of Prophet Moses, they felt confused about the existence of human qualities in these prophets, which constitute a veil on their perfect beauty, and thus entertained doubts about them. The trouble was that they did not recognise the reality behind the Divine Administration which required that prophets should be raised. What they thought – and were familiar with – was that the prophets should be like Him who has sent them. Therefore, they considered prophets in human forms something very remote and unbelievable, and to support their contention they talked of doubts, weak and not worth listening. For example they asked how a man who needed food and drink could be a prophet. Why did not God send an angel for this purpose? Why did He not send revelation to every person individually? If you ponder a little and take true the picture, which has been drawn of the conditions, creeds, and actions of the Polytheists, then you better take into consideration the conditions of the people of these times, particularly of those living on the borders of the Muslim countries. They have brought many changes and think exceedingly high of the cult of sainthood (Wilāyat). Inspite of the fact that they recognise this trait in the ancient saints, they consider the existence of such saints an impossibility in the present age. They visit their graves and tombs, and indulge in many forms of polytheism. Are they not considerably given over to Anthropomorphism and Change? It has been stated in a sound Tradition that 'you will surely follow in the footsteps of those who have gone before you', and it appropriately applies to the Muslim community of the present days, involved as it is in various acts of evil and corrupt beliefs. May God protect us from this.[1]

In short, God, out of His mercy, raised the Holy Prophet from among the Arabs and commanded him to establish the Ḥānāfi creed (Religion of Abraham). In the Qur'ān, God disputed with the Polytheists, and in disputation reasoned with them on the basis of their own accepted principles – which were from the remnants of Hānāfi creed – so that a firm argument could be established against them. Thus the answer to the practised Polytheism was, firstly, to demand from them the proof of what they believed and did, and the reason why they deviated from the faith and practices of their forefathers; and secondly, to show to them the non-existence of equality between the Creator and the created, upholding that God alone was entitled to the extreme reverence. Thirdly, it was also intended to let the Polytheists know that all prophets were unanimous on this issue, as is stated in the Holy Qur'ān, "We have not sent before any messenger but had revealed to him that there is no god but I, so worship Me alone"![2] Fourthly God exposed to them the odiousness of the worship of idols, and pointed to them how far below were these stone idols to human beings, what to speak of their position in comparison to that of Divinity. This answer is given to people who had taken the stone as Deity.

The answer for their anthropomorphism was given firstly, by demanding from them the proof of it, and by asking them why did they break their faith in the practice of their forefathers. Secondly, they were told that it was necessary, in that case, that both the father and the son be of the one and the same species, and that the sameness did not exist. Thirdly, they were shown the ugliness of their actions in trying to prove as belonging to God what they did not like for themselves. God says in the Qur'ān "What, you set up

1. Trimidhī Vol. II — حدثنا سعيد بن عبد الرحمٰن . . . ، فقال النبي والذى نفسى بيده لتركبن سنة من كان قبلكم
2. Sūrah Al-Anbijā, V. 25

daughters for God and sons for yourselves"![1] This kind of answer was meant particularly for those people who had the habit of accepting widely-known and merely imaginary poetic expressions. Such was the condition of most of them.

The answer to the changes (effected by them in the Divine scripture) was that the meanings which they drew were not mentioned by the scholars of their own religion. It was further explained to them that what they had indulged in was simply an innovation and the creation of those who were not infallible.

In answer to their view that Resurrection and Gathering were unbelievable, they were told, firstly, to judge the reanimation of the dead on the basis of bringing back to life the dead earth (when rain falls on it), and then to realise that it was possible and within God's power. to bring the dead to life. Secondly, they were told that to give information about them (Resurrection and Gathering) was in conformity with the practice of the people of the Divine Books.

The answer to their view in considering the Holy Prophet's mission as something remote was given, firstly, by telling them that such a mission as has been revealed in the Qur'ān did exist with the previous prophets too. "We have not sent before you any but persons with a revelation to them and those who disbelieved used to say that you are not a messenger. Tell them that God is enough as a witness between you and me and with Him is the knowledge of the Book".[2] Secondly, this view of theirs was rejected by telling them that it (the mission) meant the revelation as mentioned in the Qur'ān. "You say that I am also a human being like unto you, but to me has been made the revelation".[3] God removed their doubts by explaining how such a revelation was possible. "It does not befit a human being that God speak to him except by means of a revelation".[4] Thirdly, it was made clear to them that non-appearance of such miracles as they

1. Sūrah Al-Sāfāt, V. 149.
2. Sūrah Al-Ra'ad, V. 43
3. Sūrah Al-Kahf, V. 110
4. Sūrah Al-Shūrā, V. 51

insisted upon, of God's not agreeing to them in appointing a particular person to receive revelation as was desired by them, and for His not sending an angel as a messenger or not sending revelation to every person, were all based on the Universal Expediency which was beyond their inadequate comprehension. As the people to whom the Holy Prophet was sent were mostly Polytheists, these issues were discussed by God in a positive manner in a number of Chapters with a variety of style; no exception was made while mentioning them repeatedly. In truth, the address of the Absolute Wise in relation to these ignorant and unintelligent people should be of this type. "This is the decree of the Powerful Wise".[1]

The Jews believed in the Pentateuch, but they erred and changed its Injunctions, both in their text and meaning. They concealed some of its verses, and very unjustly, and put something that did not belong to it. They also showed extreme religious bigotry by conniving at the bigotted manner of establishment of its injunctions and acting in accordance with them. To them, the mission of the Holy Prophet was far from being possible; their behaviour towards him was impolite they would find fault with him. Their perversion did not end here; they even passed contemptible remarks about God Himself; they would display miserliness and avarice.

It should be kept in mind that the Jews would modify the translation of Pentateuch and not the original text. This is what has been ascertained by me on the authority of Ibn Abbas.[2] By a change in the meaning is meant their corrupt interpretation; this they did by imparting a meaning different from what the verse originally denoted. In fact, this was a display of their violence and deviation from the right course.

As is commonly known, in every religion a clear distinction is made between a dissolute religious person and an unbeliever who has

1. Sūrah Yāsīn, V. 38
2. 'Abdullāh b. 'Abbās, the Holy Prophet's cousin was the real founder of the Qur'ānic exegesis. He died in Ṭā'if in the year 68/687 or according to some in the year 69 or 70.

totally rejected religion. It has been shown that the unbeliever will, forever, remain in the Hell suffering painful penalty. The sinner, however, will ultimately come out of the Hell through the intercession of the prophets. This right to salvation of one who professed a particular religion is recognised in every religion. For example, in Pentateuch this position of ultimate salvation has been assigned to the Jews and the Hebrews. The same position has been assigned for the Christians in the Bible, while in the Qur'ān, it has been given to the Muslims. However, entitlement to this position depends on belief in God and the Hereafter, obedience to the Messenger sent to them, the conformity of their conduct with the injunctions of their religion, and avoidance of practices that have been prohibited. This was not a particular religion's privilege, but the Jews held the view that every Jew or Hebrew would straightaway go to paradise; their prophets, they thought, would intercede for them and deliver them from perdition (irrespective of their actions). If at all a Jew was sent to the Hell, he would stay there only for a few days, notwithstanding that there was no injunction of the Law to lend support to such a theory, and that he had not shown proper faith in God, had no faith in the Hereafter and no belief in the mission of the prophet sent to them. This was their gross ignorance and folly.

As the Holy Qur'ān is the guardian and the protector of the Divine Books, it elucidates points of doubts and confusion most completely. It is stated in the Qur'ān: 'He who does an evil and his evil encompasses him, such are inmates of the Fire in which they will remain for ever".[1]

Besides, in every religion, Injunctions are enforced according to the requirements of the age; the customs and systems of those people were taken into consideration when the Law was made. They were then urged to stick to the Law, to continue to act according to it, have belief in it, and the truth was confined to the prescribed actions. What this really denotes is that the truth was confined to the prescribed action only for those particular times and age. Here is intended the continuation of external features and not the real one

1. Sūrah Al-Baqara, V. 81

till another prophet comes and the veil of concealment of his prophethood is removed from his face. The Jews, however, drew a wrong view from this, thinking that the abrogation of Judaism was impossible. What actually was meant by the advice (Wasiyat) given to them was to have proper faith and do good deeds; the peculiarity or privilege of that religion is out of consideration. But the Jews took the peculiarity as truth and thought that Prophet Jacob (Yaqub) had advised his children to keep to Judaism forever.

Besides, God has honoured, in every religion, the prophets and their followers with titles like "The Near (Muqarrab)". "The Beloved (Maḥbūb)", and spoken in terms of hatred about those who had denounced the religion; the word employed for this purpose was what was in common use among them. It is not, therefore, a matter of surprise if the word "son" has been used in place of "beloved". But the Jews thought the honour was solely reserved for one who is a Jew, Hebrew and Israeli. They failed to understand that it (the word of honour) related to and depended upon the (acquisition of) attributes of obedience, humbleness, and the pursuit of the right path as shown by the prophets, and on nothing else. This was how the corrupt interpretation inherited from their forefathers had settled in their minds. The Qur'ān has fully removed these doubts.

The Jews concealed the verses in many ways; some of them are listed here:

1. To protect the honour and dignity of a noble person, and to acquire an authority from him, they would conceal the real fact, so that the people do not become aware of it, give up their faith in them and start abusing them for not acting in accordance with the provisions of the verses. For example, the stoning of a fornicator was a punishment prescribed in the Pentateuch, but they had abandoned it – and also concealed this from the people – on the strength of a concensus of their religious scholars who had given up this form of punishment replacing it by flogging and blackening of the face.
2. There were verses (in the Pentateuch) which said that Hagar

(Hājira) and Ishmael (Ismāil) were given the good news of the advent of a prophet from their children, and hint was provided in those verses that a new religion would emerge; it would gain complete dissemination in the land of Hedjaz and on that account the mounts of Arafāt would echo with the cries of "Labbaik Allāhuma" (Here I am for you O, God") and people from all over the world would set out for that place. These verses are still there in the Pentateuch, but the Jews interpreted them differently. They started saying that the verses simply gave an information about the emergence of a new religion, and did not command them to profess and follow the new religion. The words often on their lips were "War is prescribed for us".[1] When they found that none listened to their weak interpretations nor accept them as correct, they advised each other to conceal this secret, and avoided manifesting before the people. To this mischief of theirs refers the Qur'ān, "They say shall you inform them of what God has disclosed to you, that they may engage you in argument about it before God?".[2] O, what an ignorant people they were! Can the bestowal of such a great favour by God upon Hagar and Ishmael and mentioning this religion in such glowing terms have a meaning other than this that they were strongly urged to adopt the religion referred to? Blessed be God. This indeed is a great lie.

3. They had the habit of fabricating lies. The reason was that their religious doctors and recluses among them had become very rigid, and gone too deep into the religious affairs. Without any apparent authority from the law-giver, they would make inferences from the injunction to pick up an expediency to the choice they had in mind. This, in turn, gave rise to the spread of corrupt inferences. They then made obedience to them (the corrupt inferences) equivalent to obedience to the original book. In addition, they upheld the unanimous opinion of their predecessors (however far it was from the truth) as a conclusive argument in their favour.

They had no authoritative. clue – except sayings of their predece-

1. ملحمة كتبت علينا
2. Sūrah Al-Baqara, V. 76

ssors – to reject the prophethood of Prophet Jesus Christ. They acted in the same way to tamper with many other injunctions. Their connivance at the establishment of the Pentateuch and open display of miserliness and avarice are fully manifest. It is the requirement of the self-commanding evil within oneself (Nafs Ammāra) which overpowers most of the people, except, of course, those whom God may like to save. The Qur'ān says: "Verily the self is always commanding to do evil save those upon whom God may have mercy". This type of vileness had produced another colour in the book (Pentateuch), because they were making utmost efforts to validate what was wrong through their corrupt interpretation showing it as religion, namely that it was the injunction of religion itself.

They considered the mission of the Holy Prophet as remote, and there were certain reasons. One was the difference in the habits and way of life of the prophets, such as reflected in the number of marriages and other similar matters. The second reason was the difference as seen in their laws (Sharāi) and the way God dealt with them. The third reason was that the Holy Prophet was raised from the family of Banū Ishmael, while his predecessors, the prophets in general belonged to the family of Israil (Jacob). Yaqub etc. The principle underlying all this is that prophethood is chiefly meant for the purification of the hearts of people and correction of their customs and forms of worship; its function is not to establish the principles of virtue and vice. Every people has its own way of worship, administration of household economy and state politics. If a prophet were to appear in a people, he would not completely throw off their customs and systems, and establish instead new ones. He could, however, discriminate among the current customs. Whatever would be found in accordance with the rules and in harmony with God's pleasure, would be left untouched, and whatever would be seen as contrary to it would undergo necessary changes.

As far as reminding people of God's blessings upon the obedient and of His punishment for the disobedient is concerned, it is also done in a way with which they were familiar. And on that account

1. Sūrah Yūsuf, V. 53

have the laws of the prophets differed. An example of this difference is like the difference found in the treatment by a physician. When he treats two patients, he gives to one a cold medicine and also suggests a cold diet, and to the other he recommends a hot medicine and a hot diet. The intention of the physician in both cases is one and the same, that is, to reform the constitution and remove what is harmfull, nothing else. It is quite likely he may prescribe a different kind of medicine and diet for the people of a particular country according to its customs and systems, and in differing seasons he may hit upon a different plan in view of their conditions. Similarly when the real physician (God) desired to treat the patients suffering from spiritual malady and to strengthen the power of their angelic faculty and remove the cause of injury, the course of His treatment differed according to the differences of the people's cutoms and according to what was popular and acceptable in that age.

In short, if you want to see a sample of the Jews (in this Muslim community) then look at the vile scholars ('Ulamā' Sūī) who have become seekers of the world. They have developed the habit of blind imitation of their predecessors and have turned away from the plain text of the Qur'ān and the Tradition. They have taken the result of unwarranted deep thinking, improper rigidity and baseless inferences of the theologians as an authority and have callously neglected the teaching of the sinless law-giver. They have taken the apocryphal traditions and the corrupt interpretations as their chief guide. You will see that they are just like the Jews.

The Christians believed in Jesus Christ. Their error was, that they had divided God in three parts, each different from the other in a certain respect but united in some other respect,. They used for them the name "Aqānīm", the persons of the Sacred Trinity. They called one as 'Father'; he was similar in meaning to the Principle (Mabda) of the universe. The other they called 'Son'; he was similar to the First emanation which was a general reality and included all the created things. The third was termed as the 'Holy Spirit' and it was similar to the Abstract intelligences ('Uqūl Mujarradah). They believed that the person (Uqnūm) of the son had put on the dress of the spirit of

Jesus. Just as the angel Gabriel had appeared in the shape of a man, similarly the son had appeared in the form of the spirit of Jesus. Thus, Jesus is God, as well as the son of God, and also a human being. Therefore, the predications (Aḥkām), both human and Divine, were applicable to him. They, in this case, held fast to portions of the Bible's text wherein the word 'son' has been mentioned and where he (Jesus) has attributed performance of some of the Divine acts to himself.

If we accept that, this is the saying of Jesus himself and of none else, our reply is, that the word son in the olden times was used in the sense of the 'beloved' the 'near' and the 'selected one'. The context of the Bible gives an abundant proof of it. The reply to the other question is, that such an attribution is made just by way of a tale. For example, when an envoy of a king says that he conquered such and such country and demolished such and such fortress, it (that exploit worked) in fact, refers to the King, as he is the real power; the envoy is simply his interpreter. It is also possible that the way of revelation to Jesus may be different. The meanings from the higher world may have been imprinted on the tablet of his heart. The angel Gabriel may not have appeared to him in the shape of a human being to inspire him with the words. Thus, on account of this imprint, the words might have been uttered by him giving an indication of the attribution of those words to him, but the truth is plain and clear.

God rejected this false belief and explained that Jesus was the servant of God, he was His pure spirit which He had puffed into the womb of the veracious Mary, and He gave him support through the Holy Spirit (Gabriel) and bestowed a speical favour on him. Taking for granted, while elucidating this attribution, that God appeared in the dress of a spirit from amongst the species of other spirits, or He had represented Himself in the form of a human being (Anthropomorphism), the unity cannot be proved but by double meaning and ambiguity. The nearest word to bear this meaning is Taqwīm (Subsistence) and the like. "Exalted is He above what the unjust say".[1]

1. Sūrah Banī Isrā'īl, V: 43

If you want to see the type of such people, then look at the children of the dervishes and the saints (in this community). They (children) think very highly about them they have gone to the extreme in this respect. "Very soon the unjust will come to know the way they are turning to".[1]

Their other error is, that they firmly believed in the murder of Jesus, but actually, a confusion had taken place in the story. They considered his elevation to the heaven as his having been killed, and have thus been narrating the wrong story from father to son. God removed that confusion in the Holy Qur'ān in these words. "They had not killed him nor crucified him but the matter had become dubious to them"[2]

The saying of Jesus mentioned in the Bible in this connection simply points to the information which he had given of the daring attempt of the Jews on his life. God provided safety to him, and he was saved from murder. As far as statement of his disciples (Ḥawāriyūn) is concerned, the cause of it too is the confusion that had thus arisen; also because they were absolutely unaware of the reality of his being raised to the heaven, as they were not familiar with such novel thing and had never heard about it before [3]

Besides, they would say that the Promised Comforter (Praclate) was the same Christ who after his murder had appeared before his disciples and advised them to stick to the Bible, they also said that, Christ had told them that, as many pretenders to prophecy would appear after him, they were, therefore, advised to accept him who mentioned his name; the rest they should reject.

The Holy Qur'ān has mentioned this. The good news given by Jesus about the Prophet to come after him tallies with our Holy Prophet, and not with the spiritual form of Jesus, because it has been said in

1. Sūrah Al-Shuarā, V. 227
2. Sūrah Al-Nisā, V. 158.
3. Hawāriyūn is an Abyessinian word which entered into Arabic with the Abyssinians in Yeman. The Arabs of Hedjaz received it from the people of Najran. Jesus Christ had selected twelve persons from among his pupils to look after the church after him.

the Bible that the comforter will stay for some good time among you, will teach knowledge and purify the hearts of the people. This view has been fully made manifest only in the case of our Holy Prophet. To mention the name of Jesus is a part of worship in the sense that one may confirm his prophethood, and not that he may call him God or the son of God.

As regards the Hypocrites, they were of two kinds as follows:

1 A group which used to utter the word of faith by their tongues while their hearts were obsessed with unbelief and categorical denial of the truth. In relation to them is said, "They will be in the lowest bottom of the Hell".[1]

2. A group which had embraced Islam but had a weak faith. They still followed the customs and systems of their community. If the community were to become Muslim, they would also become Muslims, but if it happened to remain without faith, they too would remain unbelievers. Further the charms and luxuries of life had completely occupied their hearts and no place was left there for the love of God and His Prophet. Avarice, jealousy, rancour etc, had gained full control of them, with the result that their hearts found no pleasure in prayer and blessings of worship. Likewise, they became so much occupied with the affairs of their life as to leave for them no time and opportunity to think of the hereafter and attend to its affairs.

Many nonsensical thoughts and unterable doubts about the truth of the mission of the Holy Prophet occupied their hearts, although they had not drifted to such a limit as to throw off the rope of Islam and completely get out of it. The reason was, that they found the presence of human predications in him, and saw how Islam was dominating (by force and the use of sword) as did the worldly kings over various parts of a country. Besides, on account of love they had for their families and clans, they were exerting very hard and doing their utmost in supporting, aiding and helping them even though it all meant weakening the cause of Islam. This kind of hypocrisy is a hypocrisy in both action and behaviour. After the

1. Sūrah Al-Nisā',V. 145

death of the Holy Prophet, it is not possible to be aware of the first kind of hypocrisy as it pertains to the unseen; it is not possible to know what is in the hearts of people. The second kind of hypocrisy is, however, seen in practice frequently, particularly in this age of ours, and to it refers the Tradition "There are three vices which if found in man, makes him a real hypocrite. The first is, that he lies when he speaks. The second is, when he promises, he breaks the promise. The third is, when he disputes he acts shamelessly." The hypocrite always thinks of his belly while the true Muslim is anxious about the feeding of his horse (so as to use it in fight against the enemies of Islam)"[1] God has very clearly pointed out in the Qur'ān, actions and manners of these hypocrites and has explained many things about the two groups, so that the Muslim community may guard itself against them. If you want to see the type of such hypocrites, better go to the court of the ruling clique and then you will find how their associates give preference to their (ruling clique's) will over the will of the law-giver. There is practically no difference between those who, after having heard the sayings of the Holy Prophet directly, practised it (hypocrisy) and those of the present age who after having known the injunctions of the Holy Prophet through reliable sources have become bold enough to give preference to what is repugnant to his teachings. A group of the rationalists (M'aqūlīn) who carry sceptical views in their minds and have completely forgotten the Hereafter belongs to the same category of the hypocrites.

In short, when you read the Qur'ān, you should never think that the reference is to a certain group of people which once existed and has since passed away; you should realise that the mention is made according to the Tradition: "You will surely follow the ways of those who have gone before you"[2]. The reason is that there was not an evil in the past an example of which does not exist these days. The original purpose behind the address of the Qur'ān is, to mention the universals of the purposes behind the stories and not the particulars of such stories. This is the explanation of the beliefs of these

1. **Bukhārī, Vol. II Bāb, Idhā Khāsam Fajar.**
2. **Bukhārī, Vol. IV.** باب قول النبی صلعم لتتبعن سنن من كان قبلكم

misguided groups and the answers to their questions which I have been able to bring out in this book. God willing, it will be enough to guide the reader in understanding the meanings of the verses relating to Disputations.

Science Relating to Divine Favours and Punishments

Let it be remembered that the Qur'ān was revealed for the purification of the hearts of people, the Arabs as well as the non-Arabs, the *citizens* as well as the bedouins. The Divine wisdom, therefore required, that in reminding people of the favours of God, they should not be told more than what the majority of them had known about them, and that this matter should not be taken to further discussion and investigation. Even in the case of the Names and the Attributes of God, the explanation was given in such a way as could enable the people with their natural range of comprehension and intellect to understand without any practice and perseverance in the science of the Divine wisdom and recourse to scholastic theology. He summarily mentioned the existence of the First Principle, as this much knowledge is possessed by almost all the human beings. You will not find any community inhabiting a reformed and fairly improved country denying this fact. When it was impossible to prove the Attributes of God and ascertain their essence through deep thinking and on that account fail to be informed of the Divine attributes, then as a result they will not gain the required knowledge of the Divinity which is the most beneficial factor in purifying the hearts of people. This is why the Divine wisdom required that from among the perfect human attributes which people know very well and whose possession is commended and praised by them, some attributes may be selected and employed in place of the abstruse meanings, as human intellect does not have the range to reach the region of their sublimity. "Nothing is like Him"[1] is made an antidote for one who is suffering from the disease of the complex ignorance. Thus, He has prohibited them from proving the presence of such human attributes in God which may result in false beliefs, such as, that God has a son,

1. Sūrah Al-Shūrā,V. II

and that He weeps and loses balance of mind. If you were to think deeply, you will find it most difficult for man to walk on the main road of his un-acquired, specific sciences, and at the same time discriminate without any hindrance between these attributes and the ones which man's false imagination is likely to conceive. It is a matter which it is not possible for common people to comprehend; thus, it was but necessary that this science, of the attributes of God, may be made Divine, and the people should be disallowed from speaking about it as they wish.

For example, only those verses relating to His blessings and power have been chosen for mention which the settled people, the bedouins, the Arabs, and the non-Arabs, all could equally understand. The mention of spiritual blessings peculiar to the learned and the saints has been omitted; also no information is given of the unexpected blessings which are peculiar to the kings. He, therefore, made a mention of the heavens and the earth, and how He sends down water from the clouds, causes it to flow on the earth and, with it, brings out various fruits, corn-seeds and flowers. He further drew their attention how He inspired them with the knowledge of necessary arts and crafts and how He enabled them to create them. At many places, attention of the people has been drawn towards the change of their conditions when unexpected hardships overtake them; also how those hardships are removed from them. All these instances point out to the spiritual diseases which overtake people very often.

From among the Days of God, that is the events which God had created, when the obedient were blessed and the dis-obedient punished, He chose the narration of those ones which people had heard in general; which had already reached their ears. For example, the stories of the people of Noah 'Ād and Thamūd, which they had heard from their ancestors.[1] Similarly were referred the stories of the

1. The Prophet Noah was the father of Sām, Ḥām and Yāfith. The existing human race proceeds from him. He and his family were saved from the Deluge (Tufān).
The home of the 'Aditas was in Hadramaut, the province adjoining Yeman, on the borders of the desert named Aḥqāful Raml. They were punished for their sins by a violent wind which blew over them for seven nights and eight days continuously.
The people of Thamūd had their dwellings in North Arabia, between Hedjaz and Syria. They were destroyed for their disobedience by an earthquake with a noise of thunder.

Prophet Abraham and the prophets of Banū Ismāil with which they were familiar through their contact with the Jews for centuries. God did not mention the rare stories (which cause curiosity) with which they were not familiar; He gave no information about the punishment meted out to the Jews and others. He selected such famous stories as could be useful for them in remembering His pleasure and anger; and here too, He did not narrate the whole stories with full details. The wisdom behind it is, that when people hear an extremely moral story along with its full particulars, they are tempted to know its substance, and neglect its reminding aspect (Tadhkirah) which was the original purpose behind them. A wise man has said that ever since the people memorised the rules of the recitation of the Holy Qur'ān, they neglected the observance of humbleness in their recitation of it, and from the time the commentators plunged deep into the unravelling of remote aspects of the commentary, their knowledge of it (the science of commentary) became non-existent.

The stories which come in the Qur'ān repeatedly are: the creation of Adam from dust, prostration of the angels before him, Satan's refusal to prostrate and in consequence his having been cursed by God and his striving to seduce his (Adam's) children. The other stories relate to the Disputations which the prophets, such as Noah, Heber (Hūd), Ṣālih, Lot (Lūṭ) and Jethro (Shu'aib) had held with their people about the Unity of God, the performance of good deals and refraining from evil acts. They also inform about the refusal and obtinacy of those people, of their untenable doubts and the answers given to them by the prophets in dispelling those doubts. These stories also inform us about the Divine punishment meted out to the accursed and God's support to His Prophets and their followers. In addition to these, some other stories, have also been narrated, such as, the story of the Prophet Moses in relation to Pharoah and his followers, the story of the foolish persons of Banū Isrāil, their haughtiness and contention shown against Moses, and the punishment meted out to the wretched by God and coming of His help for Prophet Moses time after time. Then there are stories of the caliphate of prophets David (Dāwūd) and Solomon (Sulaimān), and miracles worked by them, the afflictions of Prophet Job (Ayyūb) and Jonah (Yūnus), the appearance of the Divine mercy for them and the acceptance of the prayer of Zakaria by God. Besides, there are wonderful stories of the Prophet Jesus, his birth without a father, his speaking in the cradle and the appearance of miracles and extra-ordinary works from him. These stories have been related according to the requirement of the style of the chapters (Suwar) in different ways, briefly as well as with elaboration.

The stories which have been narrated at one or two places are as under:

The elevation of Prophet Enoch (Idrīs) to heaven.

The Disputation of Prophet Abraham with Namrūd, his witnessing reanimation of a dead bird, and his son's sacrifice by him.

The story of Prophet Joseph.

The Story of birth of Prophet Moses, his being thrown into the sea, his killing of a Copt, his taking flight to Midian, his marriage there, his seeing the fire on a tree and hearing of words from it, the story of the killing of a cow and his meeting with Khidr.[1]

The story of Saul (Tālūt) and Goliath (Jālūt).
The story of Bilqis (Queen of Sheba).
The story of Alexander the Great (Dhul Qarnain).
The story of the Dwellers of the Cave.
The story of the two persons who conversed with each other.
The story of the inmates of Paradise.
The story of the three envoys of Prophet Jesus who were killed by the infidels.
The story of the companions of the Elephant.

The object in narrating these stories is not that people should know

1. Midian is a city in Egypt, on the Red sea, opposite to Tabuk, Midian is also name of a tribe as is mentioned by Yāqūt.

their substance; the real object is to divert the attention of the hearer towards the filthiness of polytheism and sinful acts, to draw his attention to God's punishment for such evildoers, to make him feel happy to hear of His help and providence for the sincere ones.

Similarly, description is given of Death and the events which are to follow it, of the condition of a dying person, his helplessness at the time, and the appearance of Paradise and Hell when he is dead.

The signs of the Resurrection mentioned are: the descent of the Prophet Jesus from the heaven to the earth, the coming of the Anti-Christ and of the Gods and Magoge. When these events have taken place there will be sounded the first blow of the trumpet which will cause universal destruction. There will then be the second blow which will bring the dead to life, resulting in the Gathering, Questioning and Answering, and the setting up of the Balance. Men will receive their scrolls of actions in their right and left hands. The believers will move to Paradise and the infidels to Hell-fire. The inmates of the Fire will contend with each other, denying that they had led the others astray, and will begin to curse one another. The believers, in particular, will be blessed with the sight of God, while the unbelievers will undergo various kinds of punishment, such as, chains, yokes for the necks, the boiling water, the pus and the tamarisk. In the like manner, God has mentioned various forms of bliss for the believers, such as, damsels (Ḥūr), palaces, flowing rivers, delicious foods, fine clothes, beautiful women and pleasant company of the dwellers of Paradise. These stories are narrated in different chapters briefly as well as in detail according to the requirement of the style of the chapters.

Science Relating to Injunctions

The general principle underlying the discussion on the Injunctions (Aḥkām) stipulates that as the Holy Prophet was raised in the Ḥānāfi creed, it became necessary that the laws of that creed be left intact, without making any radical change in the principles underlying the problems except where situation is particularised; for example, in effecting increase in durations and prescribing limits. God desired to purify the Arabs through the Holy Prophet and through them the rest of mankind. Thus, it became necessary that the matter of Holy Prophet is Sharīāt (Law) may be made relevant to the customs and practices of the Arabs. If you were to take into consideration the sum total of the laws of the Hānāfi creed and the practices of the Arabs, and then were to have a view of Holy Prophet's Law which aims at reforming and perfecting them, you will find one or the other cause underlying injunction (Ḥukm), one or the other expediency implied in every commandment and prohibition. The detailed account of this is rather lengthy and beyond the scope of this book.

In short, much lukewarmness found its way in the performance of various forms of worship, such as, the cleanliness (Ṭahārat), the prayer, the fast, the poor rate, the pilgrimage and the remembrance (Dhikra). The reason is that they had, because of their lack of knowledge differed among themselves in general, and had thus been neglectful and careless in their performance and proper establishment. The reason of this lukewarmness was, that a number of changes made by the Pagan Arabs in various acts of worship had crept in them. The Holy Qur'ān removed all this and brought about an orderliness in them. Many harmful practices combining with excesses and display of arrogance had crept in the household economy. Similarly, the rules of city and state administration were greatly upset. The Holy Qur'ān enunciated principles, set limits and fixed durations for them. In this connection, an account of the various kinds of small and great sins has been given. The problems of prayer have been mentioned briefly and the words, used are "establishment of the prayer (Iqāmat-i-Salāt)" The Holy Prophet explained in detail the meaning implied in it, saying that by the establishment of the prayer is meant building of mosques, arrangement for congregation (Jamā'it) and fixation of timings (for offering the prayer). The problems of poor-rate (Zakāt) have also been mentioned briefly. The Holy Prophet has provided full details about it. Fast has been mentioned in the chapters Al-

Baqara and Al-Hajj. An account of the Holy War (Jihād) has been given in chapters Al-Baqara and Al-Anfāl and at some other places. The penal laws (Ḥudūd) have been mentioned in chapters Al-Mā'ida and Al-Nūr. Similarly, an account of the inheritance has been given in chapter Al-Nisā' and that of marriage and divorce in chapters Al-Baqara and Al-Nisā, and at some other places.

When this form of narration, the benefit of which is available to the whole community is over, there comes an other form of narration, for example, sometimes question was put to the Holy Prophet and he gave a reply, or during an event when the believers made sacrifices of their lives as well as properties while the hypocrites showed self admiration and stinginess, God praised the believers and cursed the hypocrites holding out threats to them. Or some thing happened in which the Muslims were helped and saved from harm by the enemy. God, thus, showed favours to the Muslims and thereby reminded them of those favours. At times, a situation arose wherein a need was felt for giving a warning, a rebuke, a hint, an allusion, a command, a prohibition and denouncement. God, in this connection, revealed what pertained to it. It is, therefore, necessary for the commentator to make a mention of those stories by way of a summary. An allusion to the story of the battle of Badr is made in chapter Al-Anfāl, that of Uḥud in chapter Āl-'Imrān, that of Khandaq in chapter Al-Aḥzāb, that of Ḥudaibīyah in chapter Al-Fatḥ and that of Banū Nadir in chapter Al-Hashr. Similarly, a hint is given to the Muslims as an encouragement for the conquest of Mecca, and for undertaking an expedition towards Tabūk.[1] This is mentioned in chapter Al-Barā'at. For the fare-well pilgrimage similar suggestion is made in chapter Al-Māida. In the like manner, the story of marriage with Zainab is told in chapter Al-Aḥzāb and that of Māriyah in chapter Al-Taḥrīm.[2] The story of the lie (ufk) is narrated in chapter Al-Nūr and that of the Jinn who had heard the recitation of the Qur'ān from the Holy Prophet in chapter Al-Jinn and Al-Aḥqaf An account of the Masjid-ī-Darār is given in chapter Al-Barā'at and that of the Ascension in the beginning of chapter Banū Isrā'il. In fact, this form of narrating stories relates to the science of reminding people of days of adversity (Tadhkīr bi Ayyamillah) brought by God for the disobedient, but as the solution of the allusions depends on the hearing of the story itself, it is kept separate from the rest.

1. Badr is the name of a well, a watering-place in the south west of Medina where a battle was fought between the Muslims and the unbelieving Meccans on the 17th or 19th of Ramadān, in the second year of Hijra (623) in which the Muslims were victorious, and the victory became the cause of the spread of Islam.

Uḥud is the name of a mountain about four kilometer to the North of Medina. There a fighting took place in 624 between the Muslims and the Meccans in which the former suffered defeat, the Holy Prophet was wounded and his uncle Hamaza and some Anṣārs were martyred.

Khandaq is so named as the Holy Prophet and his Ansārs had dug trenches opposite to Madina for self-defence against the attacking Quraish whose leader was Abū Sufyān. The seige continued for 20 days without any result and the enemy returned to Mecca disappointed (627).

Ḥudaibīyah is a valley at one day's journey from Mecca. The Holy Prophet had gathered his companions there and demanded an oath of fealty from them before his talks with the Quraish for the visit of Ka'ba.

Tabūk is the name of a city on the pilgrim-road leading from Damascus to Madina and is situated mid-way between these. This city became famous because of a military expedition led by the Holy Prophet (630) to subdue the Arabs of the north.

Banū Nadīr, a Jewish tribe had its settlements near Madina. They had broken the treaty made with the Holy Prophet with the result that they were expelled and their property was distributed among the Meccan Emigrants (624).

2. Māriyah was a Copt girl, presented to the Holy Prophet by Muquaqis, a Roman governor of Egypt (629). The Holy Prophet married her and from her was blessed with his son Ibrāhīm who died in infancy.

THE SECOND CHAPTER

Meanings of Qur'ān

Let it be remembered that the Qur'ān was revealed in the language of the Arabs proper. They possessed the required taste and understood the implied meanings without any difficulty, as God has said about the Qur'ān, "And the clear Book",1 "The Qur'ān in Arabic, so that you may understand"[2] and "Its verses are unambiguous and clear"[3]. The intention of the law-giver was to avoid going deep into the interpretation of allegorical verses of the Qur'ān, in drawing the picture of the realities of God's attributes, in determining the doubtful and in the narration of the stories in minuteness. This was why the Companions asked very few questions from the Holy Prophet, very little is traceable in this connection. But when that age passed away and the non-Arabs mixed up with the Arabs, the original language became obsolete. At certain places difficulties arose in understanding the intended meanings, and a need was felt to investigate into the language and its grammar. This was followed by the course of asking questions and giving their answers, and thus were composed books on the exegesis. It, therefore, became necessary, that the points of difficulty be taken notice of summarily and explained properly, so that, while reflecting over them, there may arise no further need for explanation, and one may not be compelled to indulge in exaggeration in the elucidation of difficult points.

Thus, the failure to grasp meaning of a word is, at times, due to the use of a rare, strange word. The way to overcome this difficulty is to accept the meaning which was taken by the companions, their immediate followers and other men of learning. Sometimes, this

1. Sūrah Yūsuf,V. 1
2. Sūrah Yūsuf,V. 2
3. Sūrah Hūd, V. 1

failure arose out of lack of understanding the abrogated and the abrogating. On certain occasions, the cause of not understanding the meaning implied in the word is that the occasions of revelation of relevant verses are not known. At times the reason is the omission of the noun governing another (Muḍāf) and of the noun adjectified and the like. Sometimes the reason for not understanding the meaning is that one thing is substituted for the other, or one letter is substituted in place of another, or one noun in place of the other noun, or one verb in place of the other verb or a plural in place of the singular or a singular in place of the plural. Or it may be due to the use of the third person in place of the second person. And on some other occasions, the cause for not understanding the intended meaning is, placing as the first what deserves to be placed last and vice-versa. On certain occasions, it is due to the dispersion of the pronoun and the multiplicity of meanings intended by one word. At times, the reason for the failure to understand the intended meaning is the repetition and the amplificatin of the discourse. Sometimes the reason is the brevity and abridgement, the use of metonymy and an allusion, allegory, simile and the trope. It, therefore, behoves the commentators to remain well-informed of the reality of these things, and of some other similar cases, when beginning to write a commentary where clarification is required they should content themselves with hints and allusions.

Commentaries on Rarities of Qur'ān

The best commentary on the rarities of the Qur'ān (Gharib-ul-Qur'ān) which has reached us in the correct shape by means of Ibn: Abi Talha is one which is written by the commentator 'Abdulāh Ibn: 'Abbās.[1] Imām Bukhāri in his Sahiḥ has most probably relied upon the same sources. Next to it is reliable the commentary of Ibn: 'Abbās which has been passed on to us through Dahhāk inclusive of his (Ibn: Abbās's) answers given to the questions raised by Nāfi'b:

1. 'Alī b. Abi Talha al Hāshimī died in 143 A.H. He was the best of all the sources by which the commentary of Ibn. 'Abbās had been transmitted.

Al-Azraq.[1] Imām Suyūṭi has mentioned all the three sources in his Itqān.[2] The other commentary on the rarities is the one which Imām Bukhāri prepared on the authority of the companions, their Immediate followers and the followers of those Immediate followers. It thus looks proper for us that we may give a suitable account of the commentary on the rarities of the Qur'ān together with a narration of the occasions of revelation in the fifth chapter of this treatise and make it an independent one, so that, if one may like, it may be included in this treatise or treat as separate. People are, however, of different tastes.[3]

It is necessary to understand that the Campanions and their Immediate followers would, at times, explain the word by its necessary meaning. Then, what happened was that the latter commentators, at times, followed the old form of commentary in their researches and investigations they had made into the language and the place of its use. Our object in this treatise is simply to pursue the commentaries of the ancients as they actually were. This small book is not meant to give an account of the thorough examination and the close investigations they have carried out in this connection. Every word has a time when it is expressed and every point has an occasion on which it is discussed.

Abrogation

One of the difficult things in the science of commentary is to know which are the abrogating verses and which are the abrogated ones. This is a subject which is sufficiently discussed with considerable differences. The strong cause of this difficulty is the difference in the opinion of the ancients and the moderns about the technical meaning of the world Naskh (Abrogation). What is known from the

1. Dahhak b. Muzāhim Al-Hilālī al-Khurāsānī is entitled Abu-ul-Qāsim. He however had not met Ibn. 'Abbās. He died in 150 A.H.
   Nāfi' b. Azraq was a leader of a Khārijite sect Azraqites called after his name. He supported 'Abdullāh b. Zubair and was killed in the battle of Dulāb in 683.
2. Itqān takes a general survey of the Qur'ānic sciences, and may be regarded as an introduction to the critical study of the Qur'ān.
3. It refers to Fatḥ-ul-Khabīr Bi Mā Lā Budod Min Ḥifzihī Fī 'Ilm-il-Tafsīr, which is not included in this treatise.

investigation made into the speech of the Companions and the Followers is that they used the word abrogation in its grammatical sense, namely the removal of one thing by another, and not in the sense taken by the technicians. The meaning of abrogation, according to them, is the removal of some of the qualities of one verse by some other verse whether the removal be due to the fact that the time for acting upon the abrogated verse has come to an end or the reason may be the diversion of the speech from the unexpected meaning to the expected one, or because of the mention of some restriction which was only accidental or the reason may be the particularisation of the general or the cause be the explanation of what differentiates the textual (Manṣūṣ) and the one which is plainly analogical, or it may be due to the eradication of the pagan customs or the abrogation of the Preceding law (Sharīat). Thus, the subject of abrogaton is very vast and it stands to reasoning, and there is a scope for the difference of opinion about it. This is the reason why the commentators have taken the number of the abrogated verses to five hundred. But, if you were to think well and deeply, you will find that such verses are rather countless.

As regards the verses which, according to the technical meaning taken by the moderns, are considered as abrogated, their number is small, particularly in the light of the assessment we have made. Shaikh Jalālud Dīn Suyūti, after having considered the views of some of the learned scholars about them, has given a full statement about them in his "Itqān"[1] He has noted down the verses which are taken as abrogated by the moderns in conformity with the view of Ibn-ul-'Arabī, and brought their number to twenty approximately.[2] But I have a different opinion about some of these twenty as well.

Here, we consider Suyūti's words with our own observations on them. The verses in the chapter Al-Baqara: "It is prescribed when death approaches any of you, if he leaves any goods, that he make a

1. Jalāl-ud-Dīn Suyūtī (1445-1505 A.D.) was a scholar in the knowledge of the Qur'ān, Tradition, Law, Philosophy, Philology and rhetoric. Itqāṇ, on the Qur'ānic exegesis, is an introduction to its critical study.

2. Qadī Abū Bakr Ibn-ul-'Arabī of Seville (1151 A.D.)

bequest to parents and next of kin according to reasonable usage; this is due from the God-fearing[1] is taken as abrogated. In this connection it is said that it is abrogated by the verses relating to inheritance (Mawārith).[2] Some say, it is abrogated by the Traditions "There is no legacy for the heir".[3] Others are of the view that it is abrogated by the consensus of the opinion of the learned as is told by Ibn-ul-'Arabī. I, on my own part, say that this verse is abrogated by the verse, "God directs you as regards your children's (inheritence). . ."[4] and the Tradition, "There is no legacy for the heir" is an explanation of the abrogation.

The verse "For those who can do it is a ransom, the feeding of one that is indigent"[5] is taken by some as abrogated by the verse: "So every one of you who is present (at his home) during that month should spend it in fasting"[6]. Others are of the opinion, that it is unambiguous (Muḥkam) and Lā is understood (having preceded it). In my opinion, there is some other reason according to which the meaning of the verse is "For those who can keep fast, is a ransom which is the feeding of one that is indigent". Here the pronoun has been used before its antecedent, because, in respect of rank, the antecedent is prior and the inchoative has been brought after it as it is a noun. The pronoun here does not refer to the fast (Ṣiyām). Further, it has been used here in the masculine gender, because, by Fidyah (Ransom) is meant the fast and by food the alms of breaking the fast (Sadaqat-ul-Fiṭr). God in this verse has mentioned the Sadaqat-ul-Fiṭr after His command given for keeping the fast just as He has mentioned the Takbīrāt-il-Īd after the second verse.[7]

The verse, "permitted to you on the night of the fasts, is the approach

1. Sūrah Al-Baqara,V. 180
2. Sūrah Nisā',Vs. 11–12.
3. Bhukhārī,Vol. II Bāb: lā Wasīyat li Wārthin.
4. Sūrah Al-Nisā', V. 11
5. Sūrah Al-Baqara, V. 184
6. Sūrah Al-Baqara, V. 185
7. Sūrah Al-Baqara, V. 185 is followed by the words . . . . "and to glorify Him in that He guided you". . . . . . .

to your wives. . ."[1] is considered having abrogated the verse. "O you who believe, fasting is prescribed for you as it was prescribed to those before you"[2]. The reason is that what is required was to maintain agreement the people had already reached about the fast in this respect, namely, the forbiddance of eating and meeting with wives after sleep. This has been stated by Ibn-ul-Ārabī. He has also spoken of some other thing saying that, this verse abrogates the order relating to forbiddance of meeting with wives after sleep, and this is corroborated by the sound tradition as well. What I feel is, that the meaning of "As it was prescribed" is to effect comparison in the obligation itself (FīNafs-il-Wajūb). Thus, there is no abrogation here. It was simply to bring a change in their practice which was current among them before the promulgation of the Law (Sharī'at). We do not find any proof that the Holy Prophet had ever forbidden them to go to their wives. If we were to accept that he had actually forbidden them, then we would say that it is proved by the practice (Sunnah) and as such, that verse has been abrogated by this verse.

There is a verse: "They ask thee concerning fighting in the prohibited month"[3] This verse has been taken as abrogated by the verse: "And fight with the pagans, all together as they fight with you all togather"[4]. This has been brought out by Ibn: Jarīr on the authority of 'Aṭā'b: Maisar.[5] In my (Shāh Walīyullāh) opinion, this verse does not give an indication of the forbiddance of fighting, but rather of permissibility for it. This is like accepting the cause of the injunction and manifesting its prohibition. The meaning, therefore, is that though the fighting in the sacred months is a great sin, the mischief is a sin even greater. Thus, fighting is permissible for averting the danger of mischief. This interpretation is quite clear from the context itself.

1. Sūrah Al-Baqara, V. 187
2. Sūrah Al-Baqara, V. 183
3. Sūrah Al-Baqara,V.217
4. Sūrah Al-Tauba,V.36
5. **Abu Jafar Muhammad b. Jarar (838–923 A.D.) was born at Amul in Tabaristan, whence the name Tabari by which he is usually known. His great works are, the Tārīkh-ur-Rusul wal-Mulūk and his Tafsīr "Commentary on the Qurān".**
   Atā b. Maisar, Khurasani was strong in memory, considerably given over to fancy (wahm). He died in 134 A.H.

The verse, "Those of you who die and leave widows, they shall wait concerning themselves, four months and ten days, and should bequeath for their widows a year's maintenance and residence",[1] is thought as abrogated by the verse: "if any of you die and leave widows behind, they shall wait concerning themselves, four months and ten days."[2] The verse relating to the bequest (Waṣīyat) is abrogated by the verse in relation to inheritance, (Mīrāth). As for the residence, according to the opinion of some, it is unabrogated, while in the opinion of others, it is abrogated by the Tradition "Lā Suknā . . . ." (No residence)[3]. I (Walīyullāh) am of the view that, as Āllāma Suyūtī has mentioned, it is abrogated by the majority of the commentators. The meaning of the verse may be, that for the dying person, it is desirable and permissible to make a bequest, but it is not necessary for the woman to reside (in the house of her husband) during the period of bequest. This stand is taken by Ibn: 'Abbās and this interpretation is clear from the verse.[4]

The verse "Whether you show what is in your minds or conceal it, God calleth you to account for it" , is said as abrogated by the verse. . . . . "On no soul doth God place a burden greater than it can bear"[5] My (Walīyullāh) view in this connection is, that this is a case where the general is particularised. The succeeding verse makes the meaning clear, as by "What is in your minds" is meant the sincerity and hyprocrisy and not the thoughts of the mind over which one has no control, because the imposition (Taklīf) is not done where man has no power to bear.

The yerse "O ye who believe! Observe your duty to God with right

1. Sūrah Al-Baqara,V. 234 باب قصة فاطمة بنت قيس
2. Bukhārī,Vol. III
3. **In this case the verse would mean that for the husband, it is permissible to make a bequest for providing one year's expenditure and the residential facility for his wife, but for her it is not necessary to stay in his house for one year, but only for four months and ten days. In the light of this explanation no verse is abrogated. This has been the opinion of Ibn. 'Abbās, Bukhārī and Ibn: Taimīya.**
4. Surah, Al-Baqara, V. 284
5. Sūrah Al-Baqara, V. 286

observance"[1] is said to have been abrogated by the verse "O ye who believe, observe your duty to God as far as you may be able to do".[2] Some say, it is incontrovertible, and there is no other verse save this one in this chapter (Āl-'Imrān) by which the claim of abrogation could be held valid. I am of the opinion that the verse; "with right observance" refers to polytheism, infidelity and faith ('I'tiqād), while the verse: "As far as you may be able to do" refers to deeds. For example, if one is not able to perform ablution with water, he may do so by rubbing hands in dust (Tayammum), and one who is not able to stand in prayer, may offer it sitting. This explanation is clear from the context of the verse (Siyāq-i-Āyat). It conveys the same sense as is conveyed by the verse: "O my sons! Lo! Allah hath chosen for you the true religion, therefore die not save as men who have surrendered (unto Him)"[3]

The verse . . . . "And as far those with whom your right hands have made a covenant, give them their due"[4] is said as having been abrogated by the verse. . . "And those are akin nearer one another in the ordinance of Allah"[5] . . . Here I must state that the verse apparently means that the inheritance is intended for the clients (Mawālī), while doing good and maintaining connection are meant for the master of clientship. As such, there is no abrogation here.

The verse . . . . "And when kinsfolk and orphans and the needy are present at the division of the heritage"[6] . . . is said to have been abrogated. Some say it is not abrogated, but the people show carelessness in acting upon it. I, on my own part, say that, according to Ibn: 'Abbās it is incontrovertible and the command therein is rather desirable. This view of his has a greater strength.

The verse . . . . "As for those of your women who are guilty of lewdness"[7] . . . . is stated as abrogated by the verse . . . "The adulterer

1. Sūrah Al-'Imrān, V. 102
2. Sūrah Al-Taghābun, V. 16
3. Sūrah Al-Baqara, V. 132
4. Sūrah, Al-Nisā', V. 33
5. Sūrah, Al-Anfāl, V. 75
6. Sūrah Al-Anfāl, V. 8
7. Sūrah Al-Anfāl, V. 15

and the adulteress, scourage ye each one of them (with) a hundred stripes"[1] . . . In my opinion, there is no abrogation, rather the injunction (Ḥukm) is extended to its end. When that end came, the Holy Prophet made it clear what the promised way was. Thus, there is no abrogation here.

The verse . . . "O ye who believe! profane not Allah's monuments nor the sacred months"[2] . . . is taken as abrogated by the verse relating to the grant of permission to fight in them. I say, we do not find any Qur'ānic verse nor any sound Tradition abrogating it. The meaning of the verse is that fighting, which is usually forbidden, is strongly forbidden in the sacred Months. It is similar to what the Holy Prophet has said in his sermon that "Your blood and your property are forbidden for you as is blood-shed forbidden in this day of yours, in this month of yours, in this city of yours".[3]

The verse . . . . "if they have recourse unto thee (Muhammad) judge between them or disclaim jurisdiction"[4] . . . is considered as abrogated by the following verse" . . . "So judge between them by that which Allah has revealed"[5] . . . What I feel to be the meaning here is that if you choose to give decision, then give it according to the word of God and do not follow their low desires. The conclusion arrived at is, that it is left to us to leave the people of the Book to refer their case to their chiefs to decide according to their law in force among them or to decide their case according to our own revealed law (Sharī'at).

Again one part of the verse " . . . Or two others from another tribe"[6] . . . is said as abrogated by its other part; ". . . . O ye who believe! let there be witness between you when death draweth nigh unto one of you, at the time of bequest – two witnesses, just men from among you" . . . My view is, that the saying of Imām Aḥmad fits in

1. Sūrah Al-Nūr, V. 2
2. Sūrah Al-Mā'da, V. 2
3. Bukhārī, Vol. IV باب قول النبي صلعم لا ترجعوا بعدي كفاراً يضرب بعضكم رقاب بعض
4. Sūrah Al-Mā'ida, V. 45
5. Sūrah Al-Māi'da, V. 51
6. Sūrah Al-Māi'da, V. 109

with the apparent meaning of the verse.[1] ". . . . Or two others from another tribe". . . . according to other scholars mean that the two witnesses referred to will be from unrelated Muslims.

The verse: ". . . . If there be of you twenty steadfast they shall overcome two hundred"[2] . . . is considered abrogated by the verse that follows it: ". . . So if there be of you one hundred steadfast, they shall overcome two hundred"[3] . . . . Here I hold the same view as is held by Imām Suyūti namely, that it is abrogated.

The verse: ". . . . Go forth light-armed and heavy-armed and strive with your wealth and your lives"[4] . . . is said as abrogated by the verses relating to an excuse from fight and they are: ". . . . There is no blame on the blind"[5] . . . and the verse ". . . Not unto the weak nor unto the sick"[6] . . . . I am of the opinion, that by light (Khifāfah) is meant the least possible preparations for fighting, such as, steeds, (weapons of war,) men for service and supply of ration etc, to meet the needs; and by heavy (Thiqālah) is meant a good number of servants, of steeds,(weapons of war) etc. Thus, there is no abrogation here or we would say that here the abrogation has not been specified.

The verse: ". . . The adulterer shall not marry save an adulteress and an adulteress"[7] . . . is taken as abrogated by the verse: " . . . And marry such of you as are solitary and the pious of your slaves and maid-servants"[8] . . . I am to state that Imām Aḥmed has followed the outward meaning of the verse, while its meaning according to other scholars is, that the doer of a great sin is not fit but for the adulteress or that it is not desirable (Mustaḥab) to take the adulteress in marriage. The words of the verse, ". . . . And that is forbidden

1. Ahmad Ibn. Hanbal (780–855) was born in Baghdad, visited Syria,Yeman and Hedjaz in the search of traditions. He is one of the founders of the four schools of thought.
2. Sūrah Al-Anfāl, V. 65
3. Sūrah Al-Anfāl, V. 66
4. Sūrah Al-Baraā't, V. 41
5. Sūrah Al-Fath, V. 17
6. Sūrah Al-Baraā't, V. 91
7. Sūrah Al-Nūr, V. 3
8. Sūrah Al-Nūr, V. 32

unto believers. . ." is a hint towards adultery and polytheism. Thus, there is no abrogation here.

The verse. . . "O ye who believe! let your slaves, and those of you who have not come to puberty, ask leave of you at three times. . "[1] is taken by some as abrogated while the others hold a different view saying, that the people have neglected acting upon it. I say, that the stand taken by Ibn: 'Abbās in this connection is, that the verse is not abrogated. His stand is more proper and reliable.

The verse: . . . "It is not allowed thee to take (other) women henceforth nor that thou shouldst change them for other wives. . ."[2] is considered as abrogated by the verse". Oh Prophet (Lo! We have made lawful unto thee thy wives unto whom. . . thou hast paid their dowries. . . "[3] Here I would say that it is probable, that the abrogating verse may be prior in recitation to the abrogated verse, and this in my opinion is more weighty and clear.

The verse: ". . . O ye who believe! When ye hold conference with the messenger, offer alms before your conference"[4] is taken as abrogated by the verse that has followed it. I say that Imām Suyūti has said, that it is abrogated.

The verse". . . And if any of your wives have gone from you unto the disbelievers and afterwards ye have your turn (of triumph), then give unto those whose wives have gone the like of that which they have spent"[5] is said by some as abrogated by the verse in relation to the "Saif (Sword)"[6] and according to some by the verse relating to the Ghanimat (Booty)"[7] Some hold the view that it is incontrovertible. In my opinion also, it is incontrovertible, but this injunction is meant for peace-time and when the disbelievers are in power.

1. Sūrah Al-Nūr, V. 58
2. Sūrah Al-Ahzāb, V. 52
3. Sūrah Al-Ahzāb, V. 50
4. Sūrah Al-Mujādalah, V. 12
5. Sūrah Al-Mumtahinat,V. 12
6. Sūrah Al-Baqara,V. 193
7. Sūrah Al-Anfāl, V. 1

The verse ". . . O thou wrapped up in thy raiment, keep vigil the night long, save a little"[1] is taken as abrogated by the last verse of the same chapter. That last verse is again considered as abrogated by the prescription of the five prayers. I am of the view, that the claim to abrogation by the five prayers is not proved. The truth is, that there is a strong recommendation in the beginning of the chapter for the prayer at night while in the last verse that strong recommendation is abrogated and the simple recommendation is retained intact. Imām Suyūtī in conformity with the view of Ibn-ul-'Arabī has said that twenty one verses are abrogated inspite of the fact that there is a difference of opinion about them as well. The claim to abrogation of verses other than those mentioned above is not proved. The absence of abrogation is also proved in the verses: ". . . They ask thee concerning the prohibited months" . . . "And when kinsfolk and orphans and the needy present at the division of heritage. . . " and in the verse ". . . If they have recourse to thee, judge between them or disclaim jurisdiction".

Thus, the number of the abrogated verses is reduced to nineteen, but according to my views as expressed in my writings, the abrogation cannot be determined but in five verses only.[2]

Occasion of Revelation

The other difficult point in understanding the meaning of the Qur'ān is the occasion of revelation. The cause of this difficulty is also the difference of opinion that exists between the ancients and the moderns. What has been known by scrutinising the speech (Kalām) of the Companions and the Followers is that they did not use the word, "It is revealed about this" only for the event which had taken place during the life-time of the Holy Prophet denoting it to be the cause of the revelation of the verse concerned; they would mention what

1. Sūrah Al-Muzammil, V: 1
2. Maulānā 'Ubaidullāh Sindhi: Shāh Walīyullāh Aur Unkā Falasfa' pp. 72–73. It seems, Shāh Sāhib did not believe in abrogation in the Qur'ān. The solution of five verses, comparatively simple, is not difficult to seek. For example, the abrogating verse be taken as "more deserving" and the abrogated as "Less deserving", or we may take one as pointing to an "obligatory statute (Azīmat) and the other to "Permission" (Rukhsat).

the verse had verified whether it (event) had taken place in the life time of the Holy Prophet or occured after his death and said that "It is revealed in this connection" It is not necessary here to uphold that all restrictions should concord, what is required is that the original injunction fits in with. At times, a question was put to the Holy Prophet or something had happened in those good days and he had inferred the required injunction from a particular verse and had recited it (that verse) in that connection. They also used to say that "It was revealed in this connection". Sometimes they would say, "God has made this revelation" Or "It was revealed". This is a reference and a hint to the fact that the inference made by the Holy Prophet from the verse and the inspiration he was inspired with in respect of it at that very moment is also a kind of a revelation and a breathing (Nafth) into his mind. For that reason, it can be said, "It has been revealed". If here one were to interpret it as the repetition of revelation, that also is possible.

The modern commentators speak, in their notes on the Qur'ān, of many things which in reality have nothing to do with the occasion of revelation. For example, the Companions during their debates have quoted verses in support of their arguments. In the like manner, they would quote a verse which the Holy Prophet had recited, by way of an evidence to lend support to their speech. Sometimes, they narrated a tradition which conformed to the verse relevant to the occasion of revelation or for clarification of an ambiguity involved in the names mentioned in the verses, or in understanding the way of the articulation of the words of the Qur'ān or in knowing the excellence of the Qur'ānic chapters and verses how and why they are separated and disjoined from one another or in knowing the true picture how the Holy Prophet followed the commandment of the Qur'ān. All these in fact, have no relation whatsoever with the occasion of revelation, and it is also not a condition for the commentator to have a comprehensive knowledge of them (Occasions of revelation).

The condition fixed for the commentator is to possess the knowledge of two things:

1. To posssess the knowledge of the events referred to in the verses.

2. To have knowledge of an event by which the general is particularised, and some other similar matters. For example, he may know where departure has been made from the outward meaning of the verse. Otherwise it would be difficult to understand the object of the verses without the knowledge of those events.

It is necessary here to understand that in the Tradition have been mentioned a few stories of the prophets of the past. The lengthy stories in the narration of which the commentators take so much pains are all narrated by the learned of the People of the Book. A saying of the Holy Prophet which has come in the Sahih Bukhārī reads "Do not believe the People of the Book nor disbelieve them (with regard to the tales they tell of the people of the past")[1].

It may also be remembered that the Companions and the Followers used, to relate particular stories of the religion of the Polytheists and the Jews and their evil practices, for the purpose that their creeds and customs may become clear. Thus, when the commentators were saying "The verse has been revealed in connection with such and such" their inention in saying that was general, whether the occasion of revelation of the verse was the event mentioned or the one similar to it, or the verse might have been revealed close to the approach of that event. By manifesting the particular event their intention was not to manifest particularity of that event, but rather telling us that, it was a good picture of those universal matters. It is, therefore, obvious that their sayings differ on many occasions, each pulling to its own side (thus creating a wide range of opinions). But in reality their object is one and the same. Abū Dardāi' has made a reference to this point saying that no one can become a juris-consult unless he may not be able to apply the verse to different meanings, namely to draw different meanings from the verse.[2] In this wav, on many occasions two pictures

1. Bukhārī, Vol. IV, Bāb, Qual-un-Nabiyylā Tas'alū Ahl-il-Kitāb 'An Shai'in.
2. Abū Dardāi' al-Khazrajī al-Ansārī was one of the young Companions of the Holy Prophet. He was a great scholar of the Holy Qur'ān, was an Imām and Qadī of Damascus. He died in 652.

become clear in the Holy Qur'ān. One is the picture of the happy (Sa'īd) man, in this respect some qualities of happiness have been mentioned. The other picture is that of the unhappy (Shaqī) person, here too qualities of unhappiness have been manifested. The intention underlying this way of expression is to give an explanation of the injunctions (Aḥkām) in relation to those qualities and the actions, and not that, a particular person is being alluded. For example, the verse "And we have commanded unto man kindness towards parents. His mother bears him with reluctance and bringeth forth with reluctance."[1] After that God has mentioned two situations, one of the happy and the other of the unhappy person. Similar to this verse are the verses . . . "And when it is said unto them: What hath your Lord revealed? They say (mere) fables of the men of old".[2] and ". . . . And it is said unto those who ward off (evil) what your Lord hath revealed? They say: Good".[3] In the same way may this verse be treated, "God sets forth a parable, a city enjoying security and quiet"[4] And also the verse. . . "He it is Who did create you from a single soul and therefrom did make his mate that he might take rest".[5] and ". . . Successful indeed are the believers who are humble in their prayers"[6] and the verse ". . . and do not obey any one taking oaths recklessly"[7]

In this connection it is not necessary that those very peculiarities be found in a man, just as is mentioned in the verse: "The example of those who spend their property in the name of God, is like a seed".[8] Here it is not necessary that the seed should be of that particular quality. The object is to draw the picture of the increase of reward and nothing else. If a case conforming to it in many of the particulars or conforming to the whole of it be found, it will be a case of making necessary what should not be made necessary. At times, the doubt caused by an outward view of the statement is

1. Sūrah Al-Ahqāt, V. 15
2. Sūrah Al-Nahl, V. 24
3. Sūrah Al-Nahl, V.30
4. Sūrah Al-Nahl,V. 112
5. Sūrah Al-A'rāf,V. 189
6. Sūrah Al-Mu'minūn, V. 102
7. Sūrah, Al-Qalam, V.10
8. Sūrah, Al-Baqara, V. 261

removed of or at times, the answer is given to the question near to understanding for the purpose of elucidating the preceding speech, and not that one had asked a question in that age and had thereby caused a doubt. It happened many a time that the Companions on that occasion had brought in their speech a question for granted and mentioned the purpose in the form of a question and answer. If we were to investigate properly what they used to say, it will all be found as one speech. The order of the revelation of some verses after the others has no place therein. It is one sentence properly set in, and to break its restrictions on the basis of some rules cannot be done. At times, the Companions made a mention of precedence and succession, and in doing so their intention was the precedence and the succession of the rank. Just as once Ibn: 'Umar had said about the verse. . . "And those who treasure gold and silver"[1] . . that it was revealed before the revelation of the order verse pertaining to the poor-tax (Zakāt). When it was revealed, God made it as a purifying factor for the properties. It is known that the chapter Al-Barā'at is the last chapter that was revealed, and this verse comes in the stories which are narrated last. The poor tax was made obligatory many years before that, but the intention of Ibn-'Umar is, that the summary is prior to the elaboration in rank.

In short, what is conditional for the commentator is not beyond two things. One is knowledge of the stories of military expeditions etc, about the peculiarities of which hints have been given in the verses. So long as people are not aware of these stories they will be unable to understand facts about them. The other thing is knowledge of the benefits of restrictions and causes of rigidity shown at certain places. It all depends upon knowledge of the nature of revelation. This last subject in fact, is one of the arts of Taujīh.

Taujīh means explaining the cause of speech (Kalām). Its outcome is that at times, some ambiguity appears in a verse either due to the

1. Sūrah Al-Tauba, V. 34 ('Abullāh Ibn: 'Umar Ibn: al-Khattāb had embraced Islam with his father while he was a minor. About him the Holy Prophet said that he is a pious man. He has narrated one thousand and six hundred traditions. He died in 73 or 74 A.H).

remoteness of the picture indicated in the verse or contradictoriness in the verse itself, or because it becomes rather difficult for the beginner to understand what the verse verifies, as he has not understood benefit of the restriction. When the commentators solve these difficulties, the solution is named by them as "Taujīh (Interpretation). For example, here is a verse of the Qur'ān. "O sister of Aaron (Hārūn) . . ."[1] People had asked the Holy Prophet how Aaron could become the brother of Mary as there was a long duration of time between Prophet Moses and Prophet Jesus? It appeared the questioner had in his mind that Aaron mentioned here was the one who was the brother of Moses. The Holy Prophet gave the reply that the Banū Isr'āil used to give their children names of the pious who had gone before them. Similarly, they had put him the question how could man walk on his face on the Day of Judgment. He replied that God Who made him walk on feet in this world has the power to make him walk on his face in the other world. In the same way they once asked Ibn: 'Abbās, that in one verse it has come ". . . They will not ask each other (on the Day of Judgment)"[2] and in the other verse is mentioned . . . . "And some of them will turn to others (for questioning"[3] and thus, there seemed to be no point of agreement between the two. He replied that non-questioning will be on the Day of Judgment while the questioning among them will take place after their entry into the Paradise. In the like manner, people had asked 'Āisha that if Sa'i (Running) between Safā and Marva is made obligatory then why it is said "There is no sin"[4] . . . . She replied that some people used to avoid, it, and on that account, it has been said "There is no sin". Ḥadrat 'Umar once asked the Holy Prophet what the restriction: ". . . If you fear"[5] meant. He answered that it meant "Charity which you make in the name of God", meaning thereby that the generous do not do any wrong thing in their generosity.

1. Sūrah, Maryam, V. 28
2. Sūrah, Al-Mu'minūn, V. 101
3. Sūrah, Al-Sāfāt, Vs. 27, 50
4. Sūrah, Al-Baqara, V. 58. Safā and Merva are two hillocks in Mecca near the Ka'ba between which the pilgrims run in commemoration of the running of Hājir the mother of Imā'īl in the search of water. Before Islam, both these hillocks were a place of worship.
5. Sūrah, Al-Baqara, V. 229, Sūrah Al-Tauba. V. 28

In the same way God has not put this restriction for some thing wrong. The restriction is simply accidental. Examples of Taujīh are many and the intention is to draw the attention towards the meaning (of the verse).

It is proper that in the fifth chapter we may write down by way of revision and summary what Imām Bukhari, Imām Tirmidhī and Ḥākim have mentioned about the occasion of revelation and the interpretation of the difficult points in their commentaries on the basis of correct chain of attribution linked with the Companions and the Holy Prophet. And this we are doing for two reasons.[1] One is that the possession of this much knowledge of the Traditions is necessary for the commentator. For example, this much knowledge of the commentary of the rarities of the Qur'ān which we have mentioned, is but necessary for him. The other one is to understand that in many cases occasions of revelation have nothing to do with the understanding of the meanings of the verses, except some of the stories which have been mentioned in these three commentaries considered by the moderns as the most correct. But, Muhammad b: Ishāq Al-Kalbī has gone too far in this connection, and has narrated the one or the other story in relation to every verse.[2] According to the moderns, much of it is incorrect, and even the chain of attribution is questionable. To consider much excessiveness as a condition for writing a commentary is a clear error, and to take the meditation upon the Qur'ān as confined to the preservation of that chain is equivalent to losing one's share from the Book of God. I have no efforts but with God. On Him I rely and He is the Lord of the Great Throne.

1. Muhammad Al-Ja'fī (810–870) Bukhārī was born in Bukhara and there he died. For the study of the Tradition he visited Mecca and Madina, performed Hajj and from there he went to Egypt and travelled to some Asian countries and then prepared a correct record of traditions known as "al-Jāmi' al Sahīh".
Abū 'Īsa Tirmidhī (824–893) made extensive journeys to Khurasan, Iraq and Hedjaz for the search of Traditions. In this connection he wrote a book known "al-Jāmi", al-Sahīh". What characterises it is his critical remarks on the transmitters (رجال الأسناد) and the clarification of the points of difference between the known schools of thought.
Hākim of Nisapur the capital of Khurasan was one of the compiler of the Traditions. He died in 405 A.H.
2. Ibn: Ishāq is the writer of the first biography of the Holy Prophet (Sīrat Rasūl illāh). He died in Baghdad in the reign of Mansūr in 151 A.H.

Points of Obscurity

There are certain points which cause obscurity in the speech (Kalām), such as, the omission of some of its parts or particles. Sometimes, one is substituted by the other. On certain occasions, transposition takes place, namely the putting of something first which ought to be put last and vice-versa. At times, allegories, allusions and figurative verbs are used which portray a picture of the intended meaning in a perceptible form that may be necessary for it (that meaning). Sometimes, some consideration is shown for the employment of metonymy and the metaphor.

As far as the omission is concerned, it is of many kinds. For example, at times, the noun governing another noun (Muḍāf) and the noun qualified etc, are omitted as is seen in the verses, "Wa Lākinn-Al-Birr Man Āman" which means "Birr Man Āman", and "Wa Ātainā Thamūd-an-Nāqat Mubṣiratan", which actually means "Āyatan Mubṣiratan", and not that it (she-camel) was a seeing one and not blind.

Examples of the omission of predicate (Khabar) of "Inn", of the result (Jazā' opodosis) of the condition, of the object or that of the subject are generally seen in the Qur'ān when their consequent happens to be suggestive of their omission. Here are some such verses in which omission has taken place. "Fa Lau Shā'La Hadākum Ajma'īn" which means ". . . Lau Shā' Hidāyut-Kum La Hadākum . . . Al-Haqq Min Rabbik", and its meaning is "Hādh-Al-Haqq Min-Rabbik".

Besides, it may be remembered that at certain places, in the constructions, such as "Idh Qāl Rabbuk Lil-Malāīkat" and "Idh Qāl Mūsā ", the word 'Idh' happens to be a verbal adverb (ظرف فعلي), but it is translated to give the meaning of terror and threat. It is just like the case of a person who at times mentions the occasions of terror and the events of horror in a way neither to care for the construction of the sentence nor for its vowel marks. The reason is, that he speaks of those occasions of terror with the purpose that their picture may be printed into the mind of the hearer and he may be completely overwhelmed by them (occasions of terror). The investigation made in this connection has shown that in illustrating such an occasion of terror, search for its governing agent is not necessary.

It may be understood that the preposition (كلمه جار) is omitted in the beginning of An Masdarīyyad (أن مصدريه). This is common in the speech of the Arabs. Its meaning is بأن، لِأَن and on certain occasions وقت أن. It also may be remembered that sometimes the answer (جواب) of the condition is omitted as in the verses, "Wa Lau Tarā Idh Al-Zālimūn Fī Ghamarāt Al-Maut" and "Wa Lau Yara Al-Ladhīn Zalamū Idh Yar'aun Al-'Adhāb". But this kind of construction is employed to convey a sense of wonder and surprise. Thus there is no need to investigate into the omissions (omitted answers of the conditions).

There is a substitute (بدل) which is of diverse kinds. Sometimes a verb is substituted for another verb for various purposes. It is not the aim of this book to give an exhaustive account of those purposes. Here are some examples of it. There is a verse: ". . . . Hādhā Al-Ladhī Yadhkur Ālihatakum". Originally it was "Yasubb Ālihatakum", but because the mention of this word was hateful, it was substituted by "Yadhkur". Sometimes a noun is substituted in place of a noun as is seen in the verse "Fazallat A'nāqulum Lahā Khādi ʿin". Here in place of "Khā di'atan" is brought "Khādi ʿin", "Fa Qāmat Min Al-Qānitin" instead of "Qānitāt" At many places the conjunctive W (و) is used for the sake of emphasis (تاكيد) and connection (صلة) and not for the copulative conjunction (عطف), as we find in the verse ". . . . Idhā Waq'at Al-Wāq'at. . . Wa Kuntum Azwājan Thalā thit". Similarly, the use of the particle F (ف) is generally superfluous. The field of substitute is very vast and the examples of all of its kinds cannot be cited.

Sometimes, due to the dispersion of the pronoun, the drawing of two meanings from one word creates difficulty in understanding the intended meaning. An example of it is the verse ". . . . Wa Innahum

Laya ṣuddūna hum 'An al-Sabīl Wa Yaḥsabūn Annahum Muhtadūn". Here the pronoun implied in "Wa Innahum" refers to the devils and the one implied in "Wa Yahsabū n Annahum ' . . . refers to people.

At times, there is a dispersion in the verse. For example, there is a verse which originally requires to be mentioned after the end of the story, but what happens is that sometimes it is brought before the story itself, and the narration of the story follows. In the like manner sometimes a verse happnes to be anterior in revelation and posterior in recitation. just as is seen in the verse ". . . . Qad Narā Taqallub Wajik. . . ." is anterior in revelation while "Sayaqūl Al-Sufahā". . . . is posterior, but in recitation reverse is the case.

In short, these subjects need elaboration, but what we have mentioned is enough. If a fortunate student bears these points in his mind, he will be able during his study of the Qur'ān to understand the implied meaning without difficulty. The points which have not been mentioned, can be comprehended by him in the light of those which have been mentioned and from one explained example he can easily shift to the unexplained examples.

Let it be remembered that the unambiguous (Muhkam) is one from which the master of speech (Ahl-i-Lughat) can take only one meaning. And here the understanding of the Arabs is to be taken into account, and not the hair-splitting of the scholars of our time which is simply unreasonable, this is indeed a chronic disease that the unambiguous is made as allegorical and the known is rendered as unknown.

The allegorical (Mutashā bih) verse is one which admits of two meanings. At times, the word employed is common to two meanings. As for example, the world Lāmastum", which means both the sexual intercourse as well as touching with hand. Sometimes, there happens to be a possibility of both the copulative conjunction (عطف) and the commencement of a new sentence (استيناف) as is seen in the verse "Wa Mā 'Y'alam Ta'wīlahū Illālāh Wa Al-Rāsikhūn Fil 'Ilm.".

Allusion (Kināyah) is a figure of speech in which an injunction may be established but there may be no intention of its establishment in proper. The intention is, that the hearer may shift his attention to the thing which may be necessary for it (injunction) customarily or reasonably. For example, from the verse "Yadāh Mabsūtatān" the meaning of generosity is understood. To draw the picture of the intended meaning in the shape of a perceptible object is also a form of Allusion. The field of this figure of speech is very vast. Poetry, speeches of the Arabs, the Holy Qur'ān and the Tradition are replete with it.

The Hint (Ta'rīḍ) is a figure of speech in which though the injunction (Hukm) is general, the object is to state the condition of a particular person by mentioning some of his peculiarities, with whom the hearer may not be acquainted. In such cases, the reader of the Qur'ān always remains anxious needing to know that story. Whenever the Holy Prophet wanted to show his disapproval of the action of a particular person he would say: "Mā Bāl Aqwāmun Yaf'alūn Kadhā". There do exist such verses in the Qur'ān. For example, the verse; "Wa Mā Kān li Mu'minīn Wa lāMuminātin Idhā Qadallāh Wa Rasūlahū Amran. . ." Here are hinted Zainab and Zaid. In the verse: "WalāY'atil Ulil Fadl Minkum Wa Al-Sa'at. . ." is a hint about Abū Bakr. In such cases, people will not be able to understand the purpose behind it as long as they do not know the story.

Figurative verbs (مجازعقلي) is a form of speech in which an action is attributed to one which, in reality, is not its subject, and the thing is made an object which, in fact, is not the object. Thus, on account of similarity of the connection which exists between the two, the speaker claims that the matter is included in that particular one and is of the same genus. For example, "Banā Al-Amīr Al Qasr" . . . (Amīr built the palace), though the real architect was one who actually built (and not the Amīr). Or as is often said, "Anbat Al-Rabī Al-Baql". . . which means that the spring brought forth herbage, while as a matter of fact, it is God who brought it forth.[1]

1. Shāh Sāhib has quoted with illustrations a number of grammatical points and the figures of speech. Here only few are given. The interested reader is advised to refer to the original.

THE THIRD CHAPTER

WONDERFUL STYLE OF THE QUR'ĀN

The Holy Qur'ān was not revealed in separate sections and chapters enabling one to find each topic treated in one or the other chapter only. You should take it (the Qur'ān) as a collection of ordinances, just as worldly kings, according to the requirements of times and conditions, issue ordinances for their subjects, and after some time some other ordinances are issued in view of the changed conditions and so on, till many such ordinances are collected. A man puts them into writing and prepares a collection of them. In the same way, the Absolute King (God), for the guidance of His servants, has revealed to His Prophet a chapter, one after another, according to the requirements of times and conditions. During the days of the Holy Prophet every chapter was kept separate, but they (chapters) were not put into writing. In the reign of Abū Bakr and 'Umar all the chapters were collected in one volume under a particular arrangement and this collection was named as Muṣḥaf (Qur'ān). According to the Companions, the chapters wre divided into four classes as follows:

1. Sab'Ṭiwāl (سبع طوال). The seven long chapters (from Baqara to Taubah).
2. Mi'in (مئين). In this class every chapter consists of one hundred verses or a little more.
3. Mathānī (مَثَانِي). This class includes chapters which consist of verses less than hundred.
4. Mufaṣṣal (مُفَصَّل). This class is inclusive of chapters from Al-Ḥujurāt up to the end of the Qur'ān.

In the arrangement of the Qur'ān, two or three chapters which belong to the class of Mathānī are included into Mi'in class, because their order

(Siyāq) suited to that of Mi'īn. In some classes, another change has been made. Hedrat 'Uthmān got a few copies of the Qur'ān written according to the original order and sent them to various parts of the country for the benefit of people, so that they do not turn to any other arranged copy of it in future.

When the style of the chapters was in complete conformity with the ordinances of the Kings, then both in the beginning as well as at the end, (of the Chapters) the method of writing the letters was taken into account. For example, some of the letters commenced with the praise of God the Most High and some with the expression of the desired object, and some with the mention of the names of the sender and the addressee and some chits without any heading. Some letters happen to be long and some short. Similarly God the Most High, commenced some of the chapters with praise and glorification and some with the mention of the object aimed at. For example, He has said: "This is a book in which there is no doubt, is a guidance for the pious"[1] and then, "A chapter We have revealed and have prescribed".[2] It is just like this: "This is what such and such have agreed upon"[3] "This is the bequest such a one has made"[4] The Holy Prophet on the occasion of the truce of Ḥudaibiyah had written these words" "This is on which Muḥammad has given his decision."[5]

Some letters begin with the mention of the sender and addressee, just as, God has said in the Qur'ān, "It is a revelation from God, the Powerful, the Wise.[6] and as ". . . . A Book, the verses of which are made unambiguous. . . . "[7] This is a simile up to that where it is written, it is an ordinance issued by the king's court, or is like the one which reads: 'A declaration is made from the Royal court for the residents of such a town to the effect that' . . . . The Holy Prophet

1. Sūrah Al-Baqara, V. 1
2. Sūrah Al-Nūr, V. 1
3. هذا ما صالح فلان و فلان
4. هذا ما اوصى به فلان
5. هذا ما قاضى عليه محمد
6. Sūrah Zumar, V. 1
7. Sūrah Hūd, V. 1

had written in the beginning of one of his letters; ". . . . . From Muḥammad, the messenger of God, to Heraclius, the great leader of Rome. . . . ."[1] Some chits and letters are addressed without any heading, as for example God has said in the Qur'ān "When the hypocrites come to thee. . . ."[2] "God has indeed heard the statement of that woman who pleads with thee concerning her husband. . . ."[3] And, "O Prophet why do you hold unlawful?"[4]

The most eloquent expressions of the Arabs were their odes. While singing the amatory verses, in the beginning they would narrate the occasions of wonder and the events of Terror. This was their old practice. The same style, namely the narration of the events of wonder and terror, has been chosen in some of the chapters of the Qur'ān as well. God says "By those who arrange themselves in ranks, and so are strong in repelling (evil)".[5] And "By the winds which scatter broadcast, and by those that lift and bear the weight",[6] and "When the sun is folded up and when the stars will lose their light".[7]

Just as they used to end their letters with some comprehensive words, strange bequests, an emphasis upon following the preceding orders and holding out the threat to one who disobeys that, in the like manner, God has also completed His chapters with comprehensive words, with strong emphasis upon the obedience of His orders and holding out threat to the disobedient. Sometimes, in the middle of the chapters an eloquent expression of a very great benefit coupled with a wonderful style is brought in some kind of praise and glorification or an information about His blessings and favours. Just as, He has shown the difference that exists between the ranks of the

1. Heraclius (601–641) was the emperor of the eastern Roman empire. He could not stand against the attack of the Arab armies and was defeated in the battle of Yarmūk
2. Surah Al-Munāfiqūn, V. 1
3. Sūrah, Al-Mujādilah, V. 1
4. Sūrah, Al-Taḥrīm, V. 1
5. Sūrah, Al-Ṣāfāt, Vs. 1–2
6. Sūrah, Al-Zāriyāt, Vs. 1–2
7. Sūrah, Al-Takwīr, Vs. 1–2

من محمّد رسول الله الى هرقل عظيم الروم

Creator and the created, as is mentioned in the verse, ". . . . . And say, all praise is due to God and salutations upon His servants whom He has chosen. Is God better or those whom they take as associates with. . . . After that, He has explained the same meaning in the most eloquent terms and wonderful style in the following five verses. For example, the dispute with Banū Isrāil (children of Jacob, Ya'qūb) in the middle of the chapter Al-Baqara with the words: "O children of Isra'īl, remember my blessings which. . . ."[1] and with the same words He finished this process of dispute. Thus, this form of the beginning and the end of the dispute with the same speech (Kalām) occupies a high place as a form of eloquence. In the same way, He commenced the dispute with the People of the Book in the chapter Āl 'Imrān as is seen in the verse: "The religion acceptable to God is Islam in proper."[2] This has been done, so that, the cause of dispute be first specified and then may follow the discussion. God knows better the truth of the matter.

Just as odes are divided into couplets, similarly many of the chapters have been divided into verses. This has been the practice of God, but there is a difference between couplets and the (Qur'ānic) verses. The verses and the couplets which belong to the class of song (Nashīd verses which are recited alternately) are composed to delight both the singer and the hearer, save that, the couplets (of poetry) are subjected to the rules of prosody and rhyme which had been put into writing by Khalīl".[3]

The poets in general, have taken these rules of prosody from him, while the foundation of the Qur'ānic verses have been laid on such general measure and rhyme which resembles more to the natural order and not on the Afā'il and Tafā'il of the Prosodists and their specified rhymes, as it is an artificial and technical matter. Investigation of the factor which is common in both the couplets and the

1. Sūrah Al-Baraqa, V. 40
2. Sūrah Al-'Imrān,V. 19
3. Khalīl b. Ahmad was the inventor of Arabic prosody and the author of the first Arabic lexicon (the Kitāb-ul-Ayn) which, however he did not live to complete. He invented the metres and confined them to fifteen only. He died in 180 A.H.

verses of the Qur'ān which we have taken as similar to 'Nashīd' and then the recounting of those things which have been necessarily taken into account in the verses and which require a separate chapter, is a matter that needs elaboration. God is the grantor of support. The detailed account of that summary is, that man's sound nature is greatly charmed and pleased when it hears the well-measured and rhymed verses of an ode. When one begins to think over the causes of that charm and pleasure, he finds that the two speeches, the portions of which are in perfect harmony with each other, certainly delight and please the listener, so much so that he feels anxious to hear more of them. After that, when the other couplet, the portions of which were in harmony with the another, is recited to him and the thing he was feeling anxious about is also brought forth, his delight is increased twofold. And if both the couplets were found to be of the same rhyme his delight is increased threefold. Thus, the basis of taking delight in couplets is this secret in the old nature of man. All the people throughout the world endowed with sound nature are agreed on this principle. As the time passed, people, however, differed and their practices varied with regard to the mutual concordance of the portions of the couplets and the common conditions of their rhyme. The Arabs follow a particular rule which Khalīl has formulated and the Indians have their own course which suits their temper and taste. Similarly in every age people have adopted a particular mode and have established a particular way to follow. If we were to think over to trace the factor common in their different practices and varying courses we would come to the conclusion that it is a conjectural concordance between the portions of the couplet and nothing else.

For example, sometimes the Arabs in place of 'Mustaf'ilun' (مستفعلن) bring in 'Mafā'ilun' (مفاعلن) and 'Mufta'ilun' (مفتعلن), and in place of 'Fā'ilātun' (فاعلاتن) they use Fa'ilātun' (فعلاتن) and 'Fā'ilāt' (فاعلات), and they consider it a rule to do so. They count the concordance of the 'Ḍarb' of the first hemistich with that of the second hemistich and the concordance of the 'Ārūd' of the first hemistich with that of the second as important, and in the 'Hashw', they consider the employment of Zihāfāt as permissible.[1] The Persian poets on the contrary consider such use as a bad practice. Similarly, if the rhyme of one couplet is 'Qabūrā and that of the following one is 'Munīrā', it is taken as fair by the Arab poets unlike the Persian poets who dislike it. In the like manner, the use of one word in two hemistichs in a way that half of it be in the first hemistich and the other half in the second hemistich, is taken as right and correct by the Arabs but the Persians hold the opposite view. In short, the common factor in the verse whether it be Arabic or non-Arabic is the conjectural concordance, and not the real concordance, which delights and pleases the hearer.

The Indians have based the metres of their verse on the number of letters disregarding both vowels and consonants in the metre. This form of verse is also pleasing. We have seen some persons in the villages getting delighted and pleased by their songs. It is a form of speech in which there is a conjectural concordance between its constituents or it is a word following the rhyme (رديف) which sometimes happens to be one and sometimes more than one. They chant it as an ode is chanted and derive much pleasure from it. Every community has its own particular rule for its poetry. However, it is a fact, that people throughout the world are agreed upon the enjoyment of the sweet tunes and the melodious songs. They differ only in their manner and rule of singing.

The Greeks had invented some measures (metres) and named them as Māqamāt (مقامات), from which they had derived various sounds and prepared for themselves an art thoroughly detailed. The Indians invented six chief 'Rāgh s' (Songs) in music, and from them they formed the modes in music (Rāghnīs) which are thirty six in number.

1. The last foot of the first hemistich (مصرع) is called Ārūd (عروض) as it determines the metre; the last foot of the second hemistich is called Darb (ضرب) or "class" and it determines what sub-division of a particular metre the verse belongs. The opening foot of the verse is called "Sadr" (صدر), and the first of the second hemistich is called the "Beginning" (إبتداء), and the remaining parts are included in the general term "Hashw" (حشو) stuffing). Zihāfāt (زحافات), the poetic licenses. The poets sometimes may find themselves obliged by the exigencies of metre or rhyme to make some slight change either in the consonants of a word or in its vowels.

We have seen villagers who, quite unaware of both these technicalities, have formed certain harmonic cadences according to their temper and taste and from them have formed certain measures which are not subject to any general or particular rules. When they sing them, the listening gathering is simply thrilled and moved. After looking at and thinking over all these differences we find that the only common factor in their verse is the conjectural concordance in its (verse's) parts and nothing else. Reason has to see the general order. It has nothing to do with the details of rhyme and metre etc; the sound nature is interested only in the melodious notes and not in the 'Ṭawīl' and 'Basīt' metres.

When God desired to speak to this handful of dust (man), He brought into consideration the general beauty and not the models liked by some and disliked by others. Thus, when He intended to speak by the manner of the people, He held to that simple principle and not to those rules of speech which change by the change of times and the taste of people. Strict adherence to the technical rules as a matter of fact, is a sign of inability and ignorance. To bring forth the general beauties without the media of those rules in a way it may not omit any grace and elegance of the expression (Bayān) is undoubtedly miraculous and magnificent (and is beyond human power). Here I am bringing out the principle which has been the practice of God in this connection.

God followed that practice, and from it I am deducing the principle and then passing on to a rule. The rule is, that God in many of the chapters of the Qur'ān has taken into consideration the sweetness of sounds and not the measures of Tawīl and Madīd, and has taken into account the cessation of breath after the letter of prolongation (Madd) at the end of the verse or where that letter is placed, and not the rules of rhyme. This general principle needs detailed account: you better listen to a part of it as that will suffice and benefit you.

The ascending and descending of breath in throat is but natural for man, as he cannot do without it. The lengthening and shortening of breath is in his power to a certain extent, if it is left to itself. then unavoidably it will have a particular prolongation. There is a pleasure in taking breath in the beginning; it then slowly and gradually begins to diminish till it disappears completely, and then the need for a fresh breath is felt. This lengthening and prolongation of the breath is something restricted by an indeterminate limit and is specified by such spread measure that the loss or excess of two or three words, nay even the loss of one third and one fourth of that specified measure, in no way affects and disturbs the measure (of lengthening of the breath). It allows the difference of number in 'Autād' and 'Asbāb' and has the scope for placing some of the 'Arkān' before others.[1] Thus, there is a measure prepared for the prolongation of breath and it (measure) has been divided into three classes. the long (Ṭawīl), the Intermediate (Mutawassit) and the short (Qasīr). As regards the long, its example is the chapter Al-Nassa' for the Intermediate, the example is seen in the chapter Al-A'rāf, while the example of the short one is illustrated in the chapters Al-Shu'arā' and Al-Dukhān.

The completion of the breath is made on that letter of prolongation (Madd) which rests on a letter. The field of this form of rhyme is wide. It is to the taste of man and he derives much pleasure from reading it repeatedly, whether that letter of prolongation be Alif (الف) at one place and W (و) at another place. And whether that last letter be Y ي at one place, M م at another place and quaf (ق) at some other place, it makes no difference. Thus, Y'alamūn, Mu'minīn and Mustaqīm are in concordance with each other. The words Khurūj, Marīj, Tahīd, Tabār, Fawāq and 'Ujāb are all based on a rule. In the like manner is the annexation of the Alif at the end of the speech. This is a rhyme, the field of which is very wide and the repetition of which is pleasant even though the rhyming letters differ. At first place it is Karīmā, at the second place it is Hadīthā and at the third place it is Basīrā. If in this case one were to take the concordance of rhyme-letter as necessary, it would

1. The constituent parts of a foot are called 'Sabab' (سبب) consisting of two letters, and 'Watad' (وتد peg) consisting of three letters.

amount to making a thing necessary which ought not to be made necessary, as is seen in the beginning of the chapters 'Mary' and 'Al-Furqān'. Similarly, the concordance of the verses on one and the same letter is pleasing as is seen in the letter M (م) in chapter 'Al-Qitāl' (Muhammad) and N (ن) in chapter Al-Rahmān.[1] In the like manner, the repetition of one and the same sentence duirng the course of a speech gives pleasure as is observed in the chapters Al-Shu'arāa', Al, Qamar, Al-Rahmān and Al-Mursalāt.

At times, to make a hint towards the pleasure of the hearer and towards the fineness of the speech, the ends of the verses at the ends of the chapters differ from the ends of the verses in the beginning of the chapter. Thus, in many of the chapters this kind of metre and rhyme as explained before, is considered important. If, for example, a word at the end of the verse is found fit to become a rhyme, it is used as such, otherwise it is joined to a sentence which may either be expressive of the favour of God (on man) or an admonition, as God says in the Qur'ān. "Wahu Wa Al-Hakīm Al-Khabīr", Wa kān Allāh 'Alīman Hakīmā," Wa kān Allāh Bi Mā T'amalūn Khabīrā", La'allakum Tattaqūn", Inn Fī Dhālik La Āyātun Li ulil-Albāb" and "Inn Fī Dhālik La Āyātun Li Qaumīn Yatafakkarūn".

1. Such repetition is seen in the old Arabic poetry. Here is poet Muhalhil's elegy (a noteable pagan poet, uncle of Imr-ul-Qais. one of the heroes who took part in the Battle of Basūs in which his brother Suhail was killed) on the murder of his brother Kulaib: Such form of repetition is found in abundance in Persian and Urdu Poetry as well.

على أن ليس عدلا من كليب　　اذا ما ضيم جيران المجير
على أن ليس عدلا من كليب　　اذا رجف العضاه من الدبور
على أن ليس عدلا من كليب　　اذا خرجت مخبأة الخدور
على أن ليس عدلا من كليب　　اذا ما اعلنت نجوى الامور
على أن ليس عدلا من كليب　　اذا خيف المخوف من الثغور
على أن ليس عدلا من كليب　　غداة تأثل الأمر الكبير
على أن ليس عدلا من كليب　　إذا ما خار جاش المستجير

At other similar places, the sublimity of style is given expression to, as is seen in the verse "Was'al Bihī Khabīrā". Some times transposition is made, namely the placing of something in the beginning, the right of which was to have been placed at the end and vice-versa. At times, reversion (قلب) is made and a new letter is introduced in the word as is seen in words like 'Ilyāsīn' and "Tūrsīnīn".

It is necessary here to remember that the flow of speech from the tongue with ease, which is either because it is proverbial or occurs repeatedly in the verses, renders the long speech quantatively equal to the short one. At times, the first sentences are shorter than the following ones, and that too makes the speech pleasing and profitable. For example, in the speech made in the verses of the Qur'ān "Khudhūs Fa Ghullūh Thūmm Al-Jahīm Sallūh Thumm Fī Silsilatin Dhafūhā Sab'ūn Dhirāan Faslukūh", the speaker has in mind that the first and the second sentences combined together are in the one pan (of the balance) and the third in the other pan (i.e. the first two are equal to the third in weight). Sometimes, there is a verse of three principles (Qawāim) as is indicated in the verse. "Yaum Tabyadd Wujūhun Wa Taswadd Wujūhun Fa Amma Al-Ladhin Iswaddat Wujuhhum. . . . Wa Amma Al-Ladhin Ibyaddat Wujuhhum". . . In such cases, usually, the first and the second principles are joined together and counted as one long verse. On certain occasions, a verse consists of two metrical feet (Fāsilat, Metrical foot) instead of one as is illustrated by :

كالزهر فى ترف والبدر فى شرف   والبحر فى كرم والدهر فى همم

At times, one verse is made much longer than the other verse. The secret behind it is, that when an excellent speech which is produced by rhyme and metre is placed in one pan of the balance, and the excellent speech which is the result of an easy expression, agrees to its natural form and is free from any alteration, is placed in the other pan of the balance, the sound nature will certainly give weight and preference to the excellence of meaning rather than to the excellence of form. Thus, one anxiety is neglected and the right of the other anxiety is duly fulfilled.

I had said in the beginning of this subject that in many of the chapters of the Qur'ān, God's practice had been that, in some of the chapters no account of this type of metre and rhyme is taken. It appears that a part of it is after the type of the address of the preachers and a part is similar to the letters of the wise. You must have heard of the night tale of the women as narrated by 'Āisha and have known of its rhymes. Some of the Qur'ānic chapters have been revealed after the fashion of the letters of the Arabs in which no consideration of anything else was made. They are like the conversation of some persons with the others, but care has been taken to see, that every speech ends with the mention of something it was required to have been ended with. The secret behind it is the principle of the Arabic language, that the pause in reading is effected where the breath comes to an end and the charm of the speech vanishes. And it looks nice to end the breath at pause marked with Madd; for this is the reason for the existing form of the verses. These are the hidden points which have been disclosed to me.

If the people were to ask as to why the subjects of the five sciences have been discussed in the Qur'ān repeatedly and why every subject is not separately discussed at one place? My reply to them is, that when the purpose is to benefit the hearer, it can be done in two ways. One way is, that the intention be to impart teaching of what is not known. There neither the hearer had known the injunction (Ḥukm) before, nor had his mind ever conceived of it. Thus, by hearing this speech, the unknown will be known to him and the inconceived will be conceived by him. The other way is, that the intention behind this teaching be to present the picture of that knowledge to the mind of the hearer, so that his pleasure increases, both his mind and heart are lost in that (knowledge), and the colour of it (knowledge) prevails upon them. It is just like the verse of poetry, after the meaning of which, we recite it time after time, and each time find pleasure, and for the sake of this pleasure, we like to recite it again and again. The Holy Qurān in regard to each one of the five sciences has brought into consideration both these ways. Thus, it took note of giving teaching of the unknown to the ignorant, and in colouring the minds of the learned with those sciences through repetition.

In many of the subjects, however, no repetition has been made, the reason being, that the second way was not desired there. It is, for this reason that in the law (Sharīāt) the command is given for repeated recitation. Mere understanding was not considered sufficient. However, this much difference is made that in many cases, generally the repetition of those problems is adopted with fresh expressions and new styles, so that, it may be more effective in the minds of the readers and more sweet to the hearts. Had there been a repetition of one and the same word, it would have been like the repetition of a litany. But in the case of the variety of expressions and the change of the styles, the mind begins to think over the point under discussion and it (point) then swiftly descends into the mind.

If they ask why these five sciences have been spread out in the chapters of the Qur'ān and no care has been taken of their proper arrangement. Why it was not done that the verses relating to the favours of God (آلاء الله) should have been mentioned and thoroughly discussed first and then those pertaining to the Days of God (ايام الله) should have been mentioned with due details? After that they both again should have been followed by the verses in relation to disputations held with the unbelievers? In reply to these questions, I would say, that though God has the power over all possibilities, in this connection, the chief factor to count is the (Divine) wisdom behind this scheme. And that wisdom is, that this form of arrangement of the Qur'ān is in conformity with the language and the style of expressions current among the Arabs to whom the Holy Prophet was sent. A hint towards this reality has been given in the verse, . . . "They would say, what ! (a Book) not in Arabic and (a messenger) an Arab?[1] Before the revelation of the Qur'ān, there was neither any Divine Book with them nor any one composed by a human being. The form of arrangement (under which every topic is discussed in a sepa-

1. Sūrah HāMīm Sajda, V. 44

rate chapter) which the writers now-a-days have invented was not known to the Arabs. If you do not believe in this, then better consider carefully the odes of the poets who had seen both the ages, pre-Islamic as well as Islamic, the epistles of the Holy Prophet and the letters of Ḥadrat 'Umar, so that, the meaning becomes clear to you. If a style contrary to their style had been employed, they would have been simply bewildered. And if something they were not familiar with had reached their ears it would have surely upset their understanding. Besides, the intention was not simply to give them the benefit, but rather to see that the benefit is always present and ready at hand and that they are favoured with it repeatedly. And this purpose is served more strongly and completely through the unarranged form of writing.

If the people ask that when the type of metre and rhyme which is greatly esteemed by the Arab poets is more sweet than the type of metre and rhyme found in the Qur'ān, then why had it not been employed? Here I would state, that the standard of sweetness differs with different people and their taste. But if it be accepted that the method adopted by the poets is more sweet, then one cannot help admitting that the invention of quite a novel form of metre and rhyme, as given out through the tongue of the Holy Prophet who was illiterate, is the clearest sign of his being the prophet. If the Qur'ān had been revealed after the fashion of the rhyme and metre employed in poetry, the unbelievers would have thought that it is a poetry which is noted and well-known in Arabia, and would not have taken it into any account. Just as when the scholars in poetry and prose desire to establish and show their superiority to and preference over their contemporaries through manifest proofs, they find out some quite a new art, and then say that who is there to produce an erotic poem and write a letter like theirs? But if they were to compose after the type of the ancients, their excellence will not be clear but to the scholars only.

If they ask about the causes for inimitability (I'jāz) of the Qur'ān, I would say that what has beer proved before us is, that there are many causes of it. The first is its wonderful style. There were certain fields for the Arabs in which they freely displayed their eloquence, and tried to outwit their contemporaries in it. The field consisted of their odes, sermons, messages and idioms. The Arabs did not know any style other than these four, nor had they the ability and power to invent the fifth one. Thus, the origination of a style different from their own styles through the tongue of the Holy Prophet, who was an illiterate, is the height of inimitability.

The second cause is the information which it has given of the past history and of the injunctions of the preceding communities which went to confirm the truth of the past Books, and this inspite of the fact, that the Holy Prophet had not received such an education.

The third cause is, that it gives information in advance about the future events. When any such event took place according to the information given, it amounted to a fresh proof of its inimitability.

The fourth cause is the eloquence of the highest kind, which it is beyond the power of a human being to produce. We who have come in the world after the first Arabs, cannot grasp the reality of that eloquence. However, this much we understand that the use of the sweet and eloquent words and sentences with such ease and flow which we find in the Qur'ān, is not found in any of the odes of the ancient and modern poets. This matter depends upon the taste, and only the master poets, can understand it well. The common people have no such taste. We also know that in the verses relating to Tadhkīr and Mukhāṣimah, the meanings at every place have been dressed in different garments according to the style of the chapters in which they have occurred, and in this is implied such rarity which is beyond the reach of our comprehension. It behoves a person who does not understand this to think over the stories of the Prophets which have been narrated in the chapters, A'rāf, Hūd and Shuarā'a, then see them again as mentioned in the chapter Sāffāt and after that, and look into them in the chapter Zāriyāt, so that the difference becomes clear to him. In the like manner, the account of the punishment of the disobedient and of the enjoyment of the obedient has been given at every place in a different form. Similarly, the narration of the story of the contention of some of the inmates of the Hell-fire with others is given at different places in quite a different manner. This, however, calls for a lengthy explanation, and this book is not meant for that.

We know that the requirement of conditions and also of metaphors and metonymys, the details of which are given in the explanatory science (such as rhetoric, oration and eloquence), is fully and completely considered in the Qur'ān, inspite of the fact, that the people addressed were illiterate and absolutely unacquainted with these arts. A consideration better than that is inconceivable. The reason is that what is desired here is, that some useful points be introduced in the known form of address with which all are acquainted, so that, both the common and the special may understand them. This is like combining the two contraries.

زفرق تا قدمش هر کجا که می نگرم   کرشمهٔ دامن دل میکشد که جا اینجا ست

There is another point as well, which can be understood only by those who deeply reflect over the secrets of Law; and that point is, that the five sciences are a clear proof of the Qur'ān's having been revealed by God for the guidance of mankind. Its example is like that of an expert physician who when looks into the Qānūn[1] and goes deep into the description given there of the causes and signs of the diseases and the properties of the drugs, will not doubt that the author of it (Qānūn) is perfect in the science of medicine. Similarly a scholar who knows the Secrets behind the injunctions of the Law, will surely understand what kind of teaching is required for the purification of the hearts of people. After that, when he thinks over the five sciences, he will certainly find that they, with respect to their meanings, have been so clearly explained that there is no need of any further explanation whatsoever.

آفتاب آمد دلیل آفتاب   گر دلیلت باید از وی رو متاب

1. A book written on medicine by Ibn: Sīnạ.

THE FOURTH CHAPTER

SCIENCE OF EXEGESIS

Here we are to discuss this science and give an account of the solution of differences found in it among the Companions and the Followers.

Let it be remembered that the commentators are of different classes; they are as follows:

(1) The commentators who had aimed at the narration of the Traditions suitable to the verses, no matter whether the Tradition narrated was Marfū'[1] or Mauqūf[2] or it was the saying of the Followers or an Isrāili news. This is the course of the Traditionists.

(2) Those who engage themselves in interpreting the verses in relation to the Divine attributes and names. If they found something in disagreement with the doctrine of transcendence (that God transcends human attributes), they divert the verses from their outward meaning and reject the views of those who dissent. This cause is followed by the dialecticians.

(3) The commentators who make inferences of the theological injunctions, and give preference to some independent judgments over the others and give replies to the objections raised by the opposition. This is the profession of the juris-consults.

(4) Those who explain and make clear the grammatical and the lexicographical points of the Qur'ān and bring evidences in abundance from the speech of the Arabs about every subject under discussion.

1. Record of a word or deed of the Prophet.
2. An Isnād going back to the Companions, but stopping short of the Prophet.

This method is adopted by the grammarians and the lexicographers.

(5) The commentators who give thorough explanation of the points of the explanatory science (rhetoric, oration, eloquence etc) and from this point of view give an appreciation of the speech of the Qur'ān. This is the line of the men of letters.

(6) Those who relate the readings of the Qur'ān which are recorded by their teachers and do not neglect anything little and small in this respect. This is the practice of the readers.

(7) There are commentators who on the strength of slightest suitability speak of the subtleties of mysticism and spirituality. This is the course of the mystics.

In short, the field of the science of exegesis is very vast and the intention of every Muslim scholar had been to understand the meanings of the Qur'ān. Every scholar went deep into this science and has spoken of according to his power of expression and the ability for comprehension, and has held fast to the school of his chosen Imām. On this account, there came vastness in the field of the science of commentary which cannot be subjected to limitation. This is the reason why countless books have been written on the science of exegesis.

There is one more class of the commentary-writers. They intended to bring all these forms of commentary together. Sometimes, the books on this science were written in the Arabic language and at times in the Persian language. They, however, differed in commentary writing in this respect; some wrote brief commentaries while the others prepared extensive ones. This is how the field of this science expanded. With the grace and support of God I have acquired some intimacy with all these sciences and have gained the understanding of many of the principles, and to a considerable extent, the consequences of the exegesis as well. And I have acquired some measure of independence and investigation in each one of its sciences similar to the independence one acquires in a particular school of thought (Mujtahid Fil Madhhab). Two, three or more aspects of this science of commentary have also been poured into my mind from the ocean of Divine grace. If you were to ask me the right thing, then let me tell you that I am a student of the Qur'ān without any intermediary, an Uwaisī of the Holy Prophet, and have benefited, without any mediation, from the K âba of goodness (God) as have I benefited myself without any intermediary from the Holy Prophet.[1]

ولو أن لي في كل منبت شعرة لسانا   لما استوفيت واجب حمده

The Traditions:

Here-below an account has been given of the Traditions as related by the Traditionists (Ahl-i-Hadīth) in their books on commentary.

Let it be remembered that among those related Traditions, there are some which pertain to the occasion of revelation. The occasion of revelation is of two kinds and they are as follows:

1. Where an event had taken place in which the faith of the believers and the hypocrisy of the hyporcites had gone under test, as it happened in the battles of Uhud and Ahzāb. There God in His revelation praised the believers and spoke ill of the hypocrites, in order that, a distinction may be made between the two parties. In this connection, many hints have been given towards those particular events. It is, therefore, necessary that some brief explanatory account of these events may be given, so that, the sequence of the speech may become clear to the reader.

2. Where the meaning of the verse is complete in its general application without feeling any need for knowing the event which had become the occasion of revelation. It is, the general order of the verse that counts and not the particular occasion. The ancient

1. Uwais al-Qarnī, is Uwais b.'Āmir surnamed Abū 'Amru al-Qarnī. He had seen the time of the Holy Prophet but had not seen him. He had embraced Islam and received inspiration from the Holy Prophet directly.

commentators with this intention that the Traditions suitable to that verse may be collected or with this aim in view that the verifier of the general application of the verse may be explained, have mentioned that event (as the cause for revelation), while as a matter of fact, there was no need of making such a reference.

What has been proved before me is, that the Companions and the Followers generally said that such and such verse was revealed in connection with such and such event. In saying so, their intention was simply to portray the picture of what that verse verifies. The mention of a particular event was made as the verse, because of its generality, had included it as well, whether that event had happened before or after its revelation, and whether it was Isrā'īlī or Jāhilī or pertained to the period of Islam, and whether it embraced all the restrictions of the verse or only some of them. All this makes no difference so far as the general application of the verse is concerned. From this investigation, it is clear that the occasion of revelation is subject to an independent inquiry. Similarly, many of the stories narrated by the commentators, relating to the occasion of revelation are also subject to scrutiny and independent judgment. If a person keeps this point in view before himself, with little effort he will be able to find out the solution of the differences which the commentators have about the occasion of revelation. There is a point which may be borne in mind in relation to the occasion of revelation.

An explanation may be given of the story to which a hint has been given in the Qur'ān. The aim of the commentators in this matter has been to give an exhaustive account of that story with all its particulars from the history of the Banū Isrā'il (but it was not necessary). Here it is required that details of the story to which a clear hint has been given in the verse may be given in a way that the knower of the language should stop and want to search and investigate the story. There, it is the duty of the commentator to make a mention of it, while it is simply useless to take pains in narrating which is extraneous to it, such as, was the cow of Banū Isrāīl male or female and was the dog of the Inmates of the cave black, white or red. The Companions used to dislike it and considered it as a sheer waste of time.

Here are two points which need to be kept in mind. One is, that the very principle in this connection is to narrate the story as it was heard without the interference of reason. What has happened is that some ancient commentators, having taken that allusion as their guide, have taken one or the other event suitable to the allusion for granted and then have narrated it in the form of probability. This is the reason why the latter commentators are confused. As the style of explanation in those days was not clear and improved, the statement made by way of probability was taken as one based on certainty, and one thing might have been taken for the other. This matter is subject to independent thinking, and there is enough scope for reason to look into it carefully. This offers a wide field for every one to pronounce views he likes. Whosoever will remember this point, will be able to give a decision about many of the differences among the commentators. He will also be in a position to understand, that in many of the discussions of the Companions, it was not necessarily their religious views which they at times expressed, but the discussions were simply held for scientific investigation which some religious scholars quote during their course of discussions. I would accord with this saying of Ibn: ʿAbbās on this matter when he says, that he finds in the Book (Qur'ān) only the wiping but people refused that and by it they meant washing.[1]

What I understand from this is, that he had not taken wiping as an obligatory duty and had not considered the verse as suggestive of wiping being a principle (Rukn).

According to me the view of Ibn: ʿĀbbās was also that of the prescription of the washing in the ablution. There he simply states a certain doubt and manifests a point of probability in order to see how the learned of this age are to effect reconciliation in this contradiction and what course they are to follow. But people who are not acquainted with the day-to-day activities of the ancients had taken this statement of Ibn Abbās as his religious views. How far away it is from the truth .

1. The saying of Ibn. ʿAbbas is.

لاأجد في كتاب الله رفامسحوبرؤسكم وأرجلكم الى الكعبين ، الاّ المسح ولكنّهم أبوا الاّ الغسل

The other point is that it has become a practice in our religion to make quotations from the stories of Banū Isrā'īl, particularly when there is a clear Tradition to the effect that "You neither believe them nor disbelieve them"[1] This is an established rule. Here are two points to be kept in view:

One is, that as long as the allusion in the Qur'ān is found to have been explained by the Tradition, one need not refer to the reports of Banū Isrā'īl. For example, as the incidence referred to in the verse, "And we did try Solomon: We placed on his throne a body (without life): but he did turn (to Us in true devotion)"[2] is found to have been mentioned in the Tradition which explains that the Prophet Solomon had neglected the mention of Inshā Allāh (If God wished) and for that, he was taken to task. Where is then the need for us to narrate the story of the Sakhrah"[3]

The other point is that a necessary thing should be mentioned according to its requirements only. One should keep this point in view and express according to the requirement of the allusion, so that, it could be confirmed with an evidence from the Qur'ān, one should avoid speaking more than that. Here is an extremely subtle point which it is necessary to understand. And the point is, that sometimes one and the same story is narrated summarily in the Holy Qur'ān at one place and with details at another place. For example, God has said at one place, "I know better what you do not know", and at some other place His words are, "Have I not told you that I know better the unseen of the heavens and the earth and I know well what you manifest and what you hide". The meaning of this verse is exactly the same as is implied in the preceding one with this exception that, in this it is expressed in some detail. The elaboration of this summary can now be understood, and, in this way, one can move on from summary to elaboration.

God, for example, in the chapter Mary, has mentioned the story of

1. Bukhārī,Vol. IV
2. Sūrah Sād,V: 34.
3. الصخرة: قبّة فى القدس بنيت سنة ٦٩١ ع

Jesus rather summarily. His words are "And we are to make him a sign for people and a mercy from Us, and it was a matter already decided"[1] In the chapter Āl-'Imrān, the detailed account has been given as is seen in the words ". . . A messenger to Banū Isrāīl. I have come to you with a sign from your Lord"[2] In these words the good news is given in detail, while in the preceding verse it is given summarily. I have inferred from this that the meaning of the verse (I have been sent) as a messenger to Banū Isrāīl is to give them the information to the effect that I have certainly come to you.[3] This verse comes in the category of good news and is not connected with something alluded, just as Imām Suyūṭī has pointed out where he has said that "When God raised him he said: I am the messenger of God to you and have certainly come to you"[4]

Then there is an explanation of the rarities; this is based on search and investigation of the language of the Arabs, so that, one may, through the pros and cons of the verse, understand the relation of the words to the constituent parts of the sentence which has been mentioned there. This point is subject to reason and there is a scope for the difference of opinion about it. The reason is that a single word in the Arabic language is used for various meanings. The scholars, in search of the use of words by the Arabs and in understanding the relation of pros and cons, differ from each other. This is why the sayings of the Companions and the Followers, in this respect, have differed, every one following his own view.

When the genuine commentator happens to comment upon the rarities, he takes two points into consideration. One point is the use of words and sentences by the Arabs, to see which aspect is stronger and more weighty in the light of their use. The other is the mutual relation of pros and cons and see which aspect is more preponderant, this after having considered the laid down principles, searched out the ways, the words and sentences used by the Arabs, and after having

1. Sūrah Mary, V. 21.
2. Sūrah Al'Imran, V. 49
3. رسولا الی بنی اسرائیل معہ انی قد جئتکم
4. فلما بعثه الله، قال انی رسول الله الیکم بانی قد جئتکم

carried out a thorough investigation into the Traditions. I, in this respect, have been able to make fresh and new inferences, the beauty of which cannot remain concealed save to one who is unjust and rough by nature. For example, there is the verse "Qiṣāṣ has been prescribed for you in the case of the Qatlā"[1]; The meaning of Qiṣāṣ according to me, is equality and by Qatlā is meant the murdered only, and we take one with the other as co-partners under one rule. By adopting this meaning one will not be dragged to take the trouble of entertaining a belief in the abrogation of this verse while translating "A female for the female", and will not make ambilogies which could disappear by little consideration. Similarly in the words, "They ask thee about Ahilla (New Moons)"[2]; the meaning of Ahilla as I understand it, is the Ashhurun (the months), the months of Hajj. This is why God said at another place that "They were the appointed times for the people and the Pilgrimage".[3] In the like manner, in the verse, "It is He who brought out those who disbelieved from among the People of the Book from their towns for "Awwal il-Hashr". [4] The words Awwal-il-Hashr here mean Awwal Jamīl-Junūd (the first gathering of the armies) as is seen at other places in the words of God", send into the cities the Hāshirīn",[5] and "for Solomon, his armies gathered (Hushir)"[6].

The other science of the Exegesis is the explanation of the abrogating and the abrogated verses. Here it is necessary to understand two points. One point is that the Companions and the Followers were using the word abrogation (Naskh) in the sense other than what is taken by the technicians. The meaning taken by them happened to be near to the idiomatic and the lexicographical meaning. Thus, the meaning of abrogation according to them was the removal of some of the attributes of the preceding verse by the succeeding one, whether that removal was due to the termination of the period of acting upon it or because the meaning taken (at the outset) in haste is diverted

1. Sūrah Al-Baqara, V. 178
2. Sūrah Al-Baqara, V. 189
3. Sūrah Al-Baqara, V. 189
4. Sūrah Al-Hashr, V. 2
5. Sūrah Al-Aʿrāf, V. 111
6. Sūrah Al-Naml, V. 17

to one which is not taken hastily; or there may have been an addition of a restriction or the general is particularised or that, there is a great difference between the real meaning implied in the text and the one taken from it outwardly. This subject is of wider scope and can be subjected to reasoning. This is the reason why the commentators have raised the number of the abrogated verses to five hundred. Even in the case of technical abrogation the rule is that necessary information should be gathered about the occasions when the verses were revealed. What has happened is that sometimes the learned have taken the unanimous opinion of the ancients and the consensus of the learned as a sign of abrogation, and thus have maintained that view. Many of the theologians have committed this mistake. It is possible that the verifier of the verse may be different from the verifier of the consensus of the learned.

The other science of the Exegesis is the narratives (Āthār) which are based on the Naskh (Abrogation). This subject is like an ocean and to reach its bottom is certainly difficult. The Traditionists, besides these things (in relation to the Exegesis) have other things in view as well which they make mention of. For example, in the discussions of the Companions about a certain problem, they quote a particular verse in evidence, or give an illustration of the problem by mentioning a certain verse. At times, they speak of the recitation done by the Holy Prophet of a particular verse and cite it as an evidence, or narrate a Tradition which may fit in with the verse in its original meaning, or mention the manner in which the word is narrated to have been articulated by the Holy Prophet and the Companions.

Inferences

One item of this science is the way of making inferences of the injunctions (Aḥkām). The field of this subject is very vast and there is a wide scope for reason to speak on the knowledge of the real meanings, the hints and the requirements of the verses, there is also enough ground for difference of opinion. The knowledge in regard to the division of these inferences into ten classes and their arrangement has been poured into my mind by God Almighty. The statement which I am to make is a great criterion for testing many of the inferred injunctions. Following are such classes:

Taujīh (توجيه): It is an art of manifold forms which the commentators have made use of in their comments on the text. By it is tested their intelligence and on that account, the difference in their degrees is manifested. The Companions, in spite of the fact that they were not acquainted with the improved rules of scrutinisation in those days, have not spoken on the ambilogy (Taujīh) of the Qur'ān. The reality of the Taujīh is, that if a commentator were to find a difficulty in understanding the speech of the author, he should stop over there and try to solve the difficulty. As the level of intelligence of the readers of the Book is not the same, the ambilogy in relation to the beginner is different from its relation to the advanced. There are certain difficulties which the advanced does not understand properly and stands in need of their solution, but the beginner is negligent of them and can have no understanding of them at all. Thus the field of speech is difficult for the initiate and not for the advanced. The advanced brings into consideration the people of varying intelligence and adopts a method suitable to the conditions of the common people, and speaks according to their intelligence. Therefore the best form of Taujīh, in the verses in relation to Mukhāsamah (Disputation), is to show that the religions of those communities do not deserve any following, also to clarify the causes of charges made against them. In the verses relating to the injunctions (Ahkām), the proper form of Taujīh is to portray the picture of the problems concerned and to mention the benefits of the (imposed) restrictions, such as, caution etc, in verses pertaining to the Āl ā'ullāh (reminding people of the bounties of God), the suitable way of Taujīh is to point the picture of the bounties of God with a mention of some of the particular occasions. In regard to the verses in connection with the Ayyāmullāh (reminding people of the punishment of God for the disobedient), the best form of it is to trace the link of some stories with the others and make abundantly clear the hints given in them (those stories). As regards the Tadhkīr-bil-Maut (reminding people of death and what is to follow), the proper form of Taujīh is to draw the picture of those events and conditions.

It is one of the forms of Taujīh to bring nearer to understanding what is remote from it, the reason being that the people are not familiar with it. Another of its form is to remove contradiction between two arguments or between two allusions or between the rational and the traditional, and to make distinction between two ambiguous cases and to effect agreement between two different statements, and to clarify the truth of the promise to which the reference had been made and to mention the manner, in which the Holy Prophet had been commanded in the Holy Qur'ān to act upon.

In short, the share of Taujīh in the commentary of the Companions is abundant and its right cannot be fulfilled so long as the cause of the difficulty is not explained fully, and an explanatory account of that difficulty is not given. After that, those sayings may be examined properly. The exaggeration in which the dialecticians have indulged while interpreting the allegorical verses and explaining the reality of the attributes of God is certainly not my profession. My profession is, after the type of one adopted by Mālik, Thaurī and Ibn: Mubārak and such other ancient learned scholars.[1] Apparently it (reality of attributes) stems from the allegorical, but the habit of going deep into it should be given up. In my opinion, it is not correct to dispute over the inferred injunctions of Law, to try to show the firmness of one's professed religion and to deceitfully attempt at offsetting the arguments of the Quran. I fear this attitude of theirs may not amount to bypassing the Qur'ān. One should always search for the indication of the verse and accept it as his religious belief, no matter whether it conforms to his already professed belief or goes against it.

1. Imam Malik b. Anas (713–795 A.D.) was born in Madina. His Muwatta is the first great corpus of the Muslim Law. He was the pioneer of the Mālikī school of thought. Sufyan Thaurī (715–778). He was one of the leading traditionalists and a learned Sufi of Iraq. His works are Al-Jami, Al-Kabiral Al Jami, Al-Saghir and Al-Far'aid.

   Abu 'Abd-ur-Rahmān 'Abdullah Ibn. Mubārak (738–798). He learnt jurisprudence from Sufyān Thāuri and Mālik. He took part in military campaign and died at Hīt in Iraq.

As regards the language of the Qur'ān, the researcher should follow its use as made by the first Arabs, and fully rely upon the sayings of the Companions and the Followers. In the syntax of the Qur'ān, a great confusion has taken place. The confusion is, that some commentators who have adopted the course of Sībwaih, when they find some point in the Qur'ān in agreement with their adopted course, begin to interpret it accordingly how-so-ever much that interpretation may be far away from reason. According to me the right course is to follow what is more strong and is fitting in with the pros and cons of the speech, no matter the view-point is of Sībawayhi or of Farrā'.[1]

In connection with the verse, "Wal-Muqīmī-nas-Salāt Wal-Mūtūn-az-zakāt", Hadrat Uthmān said, "Mustaqimul-al-'Arab Bi Alsinatihā". The truth about these words, according to me, is that a usage different from the well-known usage is also a usage. The first Arabs in their speeches have made use of many such usages which differed from the well-known rules. As the Qur'ān was revealed in the language of the first Arabs, it is not a matter of surprise if sometimes in place of W (و), Y (ى) has come, in place of the dual, singular is used and in place of the masculine, feminine is brought in. What has been proved is, that "Wal-Muqīmī-nas-Salāt" may be translated in tne nominative. God knows better.

As regards the eloquence and rhetorics, it is a separate science which flourished after the age of the Companions and the Followers. Thus, what is commonally understood by the Arabs is acceptable, while the points which are hidden and cannot be comprehended except by those who have gone very deep into that art, we do not accept them as desired and intended by the Holy Qur'ān. As regards the hints of the mystics and their considerations, they are not a part of the science of Exegesis. What happens is that while listening to the Qur'ān, some truths dawn upon the heart of the mystic. Thus, when he hears

1. These two were the celebrated grammarians of Basra and Kufa respectively. Sībawayhi was born in Basra and died in the neighbourhood of Shiraz (770). His book on grammar, entitled "The Book "Of Sībawayh", is universally celebrated. He is recognised as the leader of the school of the Basrians just as Al-Kis"ā'ī was the leader of the school of the Kufians. Al-Farrā was a pupil of Kisa'i, was a famous philologist of Kufa and died in 822 A.D.

the composition of the Qur'ānic verses and gets enshrouded in a particular state, he succeeds in gaining some gnosis. It is just like a person who when hears the story of Lailā and Majnūn, remembers his own beloved and begins to recall to his memory the moments he had once spent with her. Here is one advantage of great importance which ought to be understood, that the Holy Prophet has reckoned the science of interpretation of dreams worth consideration, and has himself followed that path, in order that, this science may be a part of his Practice for the religious scholars of the Community, and open the path for their God-given knowledge. An example of it is the verse: "Fa Ammā Man 'Atā Wat-Taqā," which has been cited by way of a simile in connection with the Predestination, though the obvious meaning of the verse is that whosoever will do these works of goodness, We will show him the way leading him to Paradise and bliss, and whosoever will do actions contrary to them, We will open for him the way leading him to Hell and torture. But, by means of an interpretation it could be understood, that every man has been created in a particular state, and that state of his will continue with him whether he understands it or not. By this intepretation, the verse is linked with the problem of Predestination. Similarly the meaning of the verse "Wa Nafsin Wa Mā Sawwāhā" is, that God apprised them of virtue and vice. but the creation of the intellectual form of virtue and vice bore resemblance to that virtue and vice summarily, when the spirits were breathed into them. Thus by this relation, this verse can also be quoted as an evidence for the problem of predestination. God knows better.

Rarities of the Qur'ān

The rarities of the Qur'ān which have been particularly mentioned in the Traditions with added importance and in reference to their excellence are of various kinds. The rarity in the science relating to Tadhkīr Bi Āl ā'illāh (Reminding people of the bounties of God) is a verse which is comprehensive in regard to the attributes of God, such as, the Āyat-ul-Kursī (The verse of Throne), the chapter Ikhlās, The ending verses of the chapter Hashr and the verses in the beginning of the chapter Mu'min.[1] The rarity in the science concerning the Tadhkīr Bi Ayyāmillāh (reminding people of the punishment by God for the disobedient) is a verse in which a story of a brief account is narrated or a known story is mentioned with full particulars, or a story of great advantage which may teach many a lesson is related. The Holy Prophet had therefore said in reference to the story of Moses and Khidr that he wished Moses had remained patient a little longer with Khidr, so that, God may have narrated the story to them in details. The rarity in the science relating to the Tadhkīr Bil Maut Wa Mā Ba'd Ān (Reminding people of the Death and what follows it) is the verse which comprises the account of the events of Resurrection etc. It has come in the Tradition that he who likes to see the Resurrection with his own eyes. should read the chapter Al-Takwīr.[2] The rarity in the science pertaining to the Injunctions (Aḥkām) is the verse which gives definition of the penal laws, the specification of a particular procedure, such as, the specification of the one hundred lashes in the case of fornication, the specification of three monthly courses or three purities (Ṭuhr) as the time of probation for the divorced or widowed woman, and the specification of the shares (of the heirs) in the heritages (Mawārith). The rarity in the science relating to the Mukhāṣimah (Disputation) is the verse, in which the course of answers is followed in such a manner as to remove the doubts by strongly convincing arguments, or the answer given is linked with explanation of the conditions of this group by a clear example, such as "Like the example of him who kindled fire' [3] Similarly, an explanation pointing out the filthiness of the worship of idols may be given, difference between the ranks of the creator and the created, the master and the slave, along with wonderful similes and examples be clearly shown and demonstrated, and the reasons for the uselessness of the deeds of the hypocrites may be convincingly stated. The rarities of the Qur'ān are not confined to these subjects only.

1. Verse of Throne, Sūrah Al-Baqara, V: 255, Ikhlās, Sūrah CXII: Al-Hashr, Sūrah LIX. Al-Mu'min Sūrah XL.
2. Al-Takwīr, Sūrah LXXXI.
3. Sūrah, Al-Baqara, V. 17

Sometimes, the rarities are implied in the eloquence of the speech and the elegance of the style. An example of it is the chapter Al-Rahmān.[1] This is the reason why in the Tradition it is named the bride of the Qur'ān. At times, the rarities are demonstrated by drawing the picture of the happy and the unhappy. It has come in the Tradition that every verse has both an outward and an inward meaning, and for everything there is a limit to know and understand.

Let it be understood that the outward of the five sciences is something which happens to be the indication and the comprehended meaning of the speech while its inward, with regard to the Tadhkīr Bi Ālā'illāh is meditating upon His bounties and contemplating upon the Deity. The rarity implied in the verses concerning Tadhkīr Bi Ayyāmillāh is to know the reasons for God's praise and blame, reward and punishment through those stories, and to learn a lesson from them. Likewise the rarity in the science relating to the Tadhkīr Bil Jannat Wan-Nār (Reminding people of the blisses of Paradise and the tortures of Hell-fire), is to manifest fear and hope and make them look as if they are seen by the eyes. The rarity of the science in relation to the verses concerning Injunctions is to draw inferences from them (Injunctions) by means of hints and suggestions. The rarity in the science pertaining to misguided groups is to have information of the origin of the abominations and connect them with other similar ones (abominations). To have information of the outward means having knowledge of the language of the Arabs and of the Traditions in connection with the Exegesis of the Qur'ān while by having the information of the inward is meant the sharpness of the intelligence, the straightness of understanding coupled with the inward light and the tranquillity of mind. God knows better.

God-given Sciences

Among sciences bestowed on me in relation to the science of commentary to which I have made references, one is the intepretation of the events which had taken place in the times of the

1. Sūrah, Al-Rahmān

prophets. In this connection, I have composed a treatise named "Tāwīl al Ahādīth"[1] By it is meant, that every event which had taken place had one or the other cause behind it, namely the capability of the Messenger and of the people he was sent to. And this was in consequence of the plan which God had desired to put into action. The other science is thorough examination of the five sciences which have been mentioned by the Qur'ān, an account of which has already been given in the beginning of this treatise. One who likes to know it, may refer to it. One other science relating to the Exegesis is the translation of the Qur'ān into the Persian language in a way it may resemble to the original Arabic in quantity, particularity, generality etc. This I have put in the "Fatḥ al Raḥmān Fī Tarjimat al-Qur'ān", but this condition has been given up at certain places from fear that the readers will not understand it without details.

There is one other science relating to the properties of the Qur'ān. Some scholars in the past have spoken on its properties in two ways. One way is similar to the prayer (Duā), while the other is like magic. I pray to God to save from it. God has opened a (new) door for me in addition to what has been narrated by them about its properties. He, once placed before me the reality of His beautiful names, the great verses and the sacred prayers and said that this was His gift given to him to make use of it as he may like. Every verse, every name and every prayer is subject to a condition which cannot come under any rule; but their rule is to wait for the instructions from the Unseen world, just as, it is done during the Istikhāra prayer, when one has to wait and see what verse or name or a hint is given to him from above.[2] Then, that verse or that name may be read in a way it is fixed by the masters of this science. This is for what I had intended to bring in this treatise. All praise is due to God in the beginning, in the end, outwardly and inwardly.

1. This book has been already translated into English by the present translator. It is published and is available in the market.
Istikhāra, the prayer of a man who has not yet made up his mind, in order to be inspired with a salutary decision regarding an intended enterprise, a journey, etc.

Abbreviated Letters

One of the sciences of the Qur'ān, the revelation of which has been made to me, is the solution of the meanings underlying the abbreviated letters of the Qur'ān. This, however, is subject to the preparation of an introduction.

Let it be remembered that the letters of the alphabet are the principles of the words of the Arabs, and each one of them has its own simple meaning, extremely fresh and modern. They cannot be interpreted without a general hint. It is here that many of the approximate words either agree in meaning or are approximate in it. For example, the scholars in literature have mentioned that where a word, N (ن) and F (ف) come together, their combination gives an indication of the meaning of going out (Khurūj) in some respect like, Nafar, Nafath, Nafah, Nafakh, Nafaq, Nafad and Nafadh. And where F (ف) and Lām (ل) combine, the combination indicates the meaning of "Opening up" like Falaq, Falah, Falaj, Faladh and Falad. It is from here that the masters in literature know that many a time the Arabs use one word in different shades of meaning by substituting approximate letters as is found in Daqq and Dakk, Walaj and Lazz.

In short, the evidences of this aspect are many. Our intention is to draw the attention of the reader and nothing else. This is the language of all Arabs, even though the pure Arabs may not be able to ascertain it and the grammarians may not be able to understand it, just as, for example, they do not know the meaning of the definition of the genus and the peculiarities of the constructions. If you ask the pure Arabs to explain what they actually are, they will not be able to explain even though they are using the same constructions in their conversation. Then, even those who are engaged in ascertaining the speech of the Arabs, are not of one and the same rank. Some are more sharp-minded than others, and besides, there are certain meanings which some of them understand thoroughly, while others do not. This also is the science of the language of the Arabs. Many of those who have studied it minutely have fallen short of understanding its (language's) intended meanings.

The abbreviated letters are the names of the chapters (Suwar) in the sense, that they summarily indicate what the chapters consist of in details. This is just like the name they fix for a book, so that its gist may become clear before the mind of the reader. As for example, Imām Bukhārī has named his book "Jāmi'-al-Sahīh al-Musnad Fī Hadīth Rasūlillāh".

The meaning of A,L,M (الٓمٓ) is, that the unspecified unseen is specified in relation to the visible world which is defiled. The reason is that both Hamza (ءَ) and h (ه) give the meaning of the unseen, save that, H is the unseen of this world while the Hamza is the unseen of the abstract world. It is, therefore, that at the time of interrogation and the conjunction ('Atif) they (Arabs) say 'Au, 'Am' (أَمْ - أَوْ), the reason being, that an affair set right by it is disturbed. And it is the unseen in relation to the specified. In the same way what makes them hesitate in it is an Unseen. In the beginning they add interrogative Hamza so that, it may indicate that the picture is gained in their minds, the details of which are such and such. They have chosen H in their mind, because it is an unseen of this world. And the specified has, in short, gained a summary, L (ل)gives the meaning of specification. It is, therefore, that at the time of making a common noun proper one L (ل) of introduction (Ta'rif) is added. When M and L (م - ل) meet together, their combination gives an indication of the defiled matter in which various realities are collected and have become restricted. And because of the requirement of the abstract, they are subjected to restriction and space.

Thus A,L,M (الٓمٓ) alludes to the simple grace which has come down in the world of space according to the customs of people, and in consequence, their sciences ('Ulūm) became specified. It fought against the hardness of their hearts by means of reminding, and for them struck against their corrupt sayings and useless actions by show of love and has the prescription of the limits of virtue and vice. The whole chapter is the explanation of it.

A,L,R (الـر) is like A,L,M (الـم) save that, R (ر) points out to hesitation, namely, that the unseen which is specified by defilement has come with defilement the second time and became specified.

M (م) also gives the same sense and alludes to the sciences which are frequently striking hard against the foul acts of the people, and that is true, as is seen in the stories of the prophets and their discourses time after time and in their repeated questions and answers. T (ط) and S (ص), both suggest an upward movement from the dirty world to the higher world, save that, T points to greatness and glory or to the ugliness and dirtiness of that moving thing while S (ص) gives the meaning of purity (Safā') and fineness.

S(س) gives the sense of penetration and its disappearance and its dispersion throughout the world. Thus T (ط) refers to the stations of the prophets, which are the marks of their paying attention to the higher world, so that an unseen picture may be created. In this world, they are mentioned in the Divine books and their account is given in general terms.

T,S,M (طسم) signifies the stations of the Prophets which are the marks of their upward movement and which have penetrated and spread throughout the dirty world.

H (ح) is similar to H (ه), the meaning of which has been already given, save that, when it possesses shining light, makes appearance and discriminates, it is interpreted as H (ح). Thus, the meaning of H,M (حم) is a brightly shining generality which is connected with the characteristics of the world defiled by false beliefs and corrupt actions. This is an allusion to the rejection of their (People's) works, and it also gives the meaning of the appearance of the truth in places of doubt, disputations and in their customs.

'A (ع) points to the appearance of the shining light and its specification.

Q (ق) is like M (م) and points to this world but from the point of power and severity.

M (م), because of the collecton and the piling up of the forms in it, signifies the extremely shining love of the Real which pervades the ugly world.

N (ن), means light which penetrates the darkness and is dispersed like a state that is seen at the time of true dawn or near the time of the setting of the sun.

Y (ي), is similar to it, save that, there is less light in it in relation to N (ن), and is specified in a lesser degree in relation to H (ح).

Thus, Yāsīn (يٓس) is an allusion to meanings which are spread in the world.

S (ص), signifies an aspect which appeared near the time of concentration of prophets upon their creator both by nature and acquisition.

Q (ق) conveys the meaning of power, severity and force which are specified in this world. It is like one who says that the object of his intention is the aspect which is created in the world by force and stroke.

K (ك), is like Q (ق), save that, its power is understood to be less than what is implied in Q.

Thus K,H,Y,Ā,S, (كهيٰعص), conveys the meaning of an ugly dark world in which, sciences some shining brightly and others dimly, are specified at the time of their return to the Creator.

In short, the meanings of these letters have been explained to me by way of taste (Dhauq). It is not possible to say more than these words which have been recorded in this book in general meanings. These words are not sufficient to explain their depth and they differ from each other in one respect or the other. God knows better the true thing.

Shāh Walīullāh composed verses both in Arabic and Persian when occasion so required. Here are quoted some of his verses in Persian which he composed at the instance of his friends and has also explained their mystical meaning.[1]

دلی دارم زخود خالی حبابش میتوان گفتن
درو کیفیتی جوش شرابش میتوان گفتن
وجودی نمود معنی ما دیدنی دارد
درین سیر نگهای بوی گلابش میتوان گفتن
سویدا دل ما یالی اندر پیچ و تاب او
نقوش عالم ام الکتابش میتوان گفتن
فرو پاشید از هم کثرت موهوم چون شبنم
زفیض معنی ما آفتابش میتوان گفتن

1. Kalimāt-i-Tayyibāt p. 191
In the first two couplets, there is a wonderful hint to a state in which the soul is attracted towards annihilating the ego. The third couplet gives the meaning of the comprehensiveness of the Pure Intellect, while the last couplet suggests the annihilation of ego which takes place when the meaning of the Pure Intellect makes an appearance.

BISHARAT

Here is an English version of a Bisharat (true dream) seen by Wān Mūsā,[1] a Malaysian scholar and a faithful disciple of late Maulānā Ūbaidullāh Sindhi, who was known to be the chief exponent of the philosophy of Shāh Walīyullāh. The Bishārat was related to this writer by another Malaysian scholar and a friend, Mr. Azīz Ahmed, who, while returning from Europe, stayed in Pakistan as guest of the writer. The Bishārat runs: "I dreamt one night, while in a state of high fever, that I was in the Holy Prophet's Mosque which was thronged by his companions. A door opened, and I saw the Holy Prophet standing there in a black cloak and white turban; I just found myself in his presence reclining on my shoulder and sitting there as if before a foreign emperor. Thus spoke the Holy Prophet to me. 'O, Mūsā, Abide by the Word of God and by my Practice, and establish them for your children and countrymen. God will in return include you and your children amongst those near Him. The Path of Shāh Walīyullāh which is being taught to your children by their teacher is my Path and my upright Practice'. I asked in wonderment, 'Prophet of God, I have heard that the traditionists have their own ways, varied and various, although all traditions are part of your Practice'. The Holy Prophet said: "The way of Shāh Walīyullāh is my Practice which I had taught to my companions and they to those who followed them and the followers to those who followed them. Then there occurred a change in the people's mind and the true path became obscure from them till God made an inspiration of this path, through me, to Shāh Walīyullāh'."

1. Hājī Wān Mūsā was known to be a scholar (alim) possessing sound knoledge of religious science. He had a sharp temper, but despite that he was willing always to retract from his opinion in the interest of truth. With his modesty and piety was combined the courage to refuse to follow instructions of others – even the bidding of a ruling Sultan if they appeared in conflict with the Law of God and the teachings of the Holy Prophet. It was this stubborness of his which later became the cause of a turning point in his life (Ref. Kelantan, edited by William R. Roff p. 156).

INDEX

D

E

F

G

H

I

INDEX

INDEX